INTRODUCING
ISSUES WITH
OPPOSING
VIEWPOINTS®

National Security

Lauri S. Friedman, *Book Editor*

GREENHAVEN PRESS
A part of Gale, Cengage Learning

GALE
CENGAGE Learning™

Detroit • New York • San Francisco • New Haven, Conn • Waterville, Maine • London

Christine Nasso, *Publisher*
Elizabeth Des Chenes, *Managing Editor*

© 2010 Greenhaven Press, a part of Gale, Cengage Learning

Gale and Greenhaven Press are registered trademarks used herein under license.

For more information, contact:
Greenhaven Press
27500 Drake Rd.
Farmington Hills, MI 48331-3535
Or you can visit our Internet site at gale.cengage.com

For product information and technology assistance, contact us at

Gale Customer Support, 1-800-877-4253
For permission to use material from this text or product, submit all requests online at www.cengage.com/permissions

Further permissions questions can be e-mailed to permissionrequest@cengage.com

Articles in Greenhaven Press anthologies are often edited for length to meet page require-ments. In addition, original titles of these works are changed to clearly present the main thesis and to explicitly indicate the author's opinion. Every effort is made to ensure that Greenhaven Press accurately reflects the original intent of the authors. Every effort has been made to trace the owners of copyrighted material.

Cover image © George Steinmetz/Corbis

LIBRARY OF CONGRESS CATALOGING-IN-PUBLICATION DATA

National security / Lauri S. Friedman, book editor.
     p. cm. -- (Introducing issues with opposing viewpoints)
   Includes bibliographical references and index.
   ISBN 978-0-7377-4481-1 (hardcover)
   1. National security--United States. 2. National security--Study and teaching--United States. I. Friedman, Lauri S.
   UA23.N247726 2009
   355'.033073--dc22
                                                                2009027495

Printed in the United States of America
1 2 3 4 5 6 7 13 12 11 10 09

Contents

Chapter 3: How Should National Security Be Balanced with Civil Liberties?

Foreword

Indulging in a wide spectrum of ideas, beliefs, and perspectives is a critical cornerstone of democracy. After all, it is often debates over differences of opinion, such as whether to legalize abortion, how to treat prisoners, or when to enact the death penalty, that shape our society and drive it forward. Such diversity of thought is frequently regarded as the hallmark of a healthy and civilized culture. As the Reverend Clifford Schutjer of the First Congregational Church in Mansfield, Ohio, declared in a 2001 sermon, "Surrounding oneself with only like-minded people, restricting what we listen to or read only to what we find agreeable is irresponsible. Refusing to entertain doubts once we make up our minds is a subtle but deadly form of arrogance." With this advice in mind, Introducing Issues with Opposing Viewpoints books aim to open readers' minds to the critically divergent views that comprise our world's most important debates.

Introducing Issues with Opposing Viewpoints simplifies for students the enormous and often overwhelming mass of material now available via print and electronic media. Collected in every volume is an array of opinions that captures the essence of a particular controversy or topic. Introducing Issues with Opposing Viewpoints books embody the spirit of nineteenth-century journalist Charles A. Dana's axiom: "Fight for your opinions, but do not believe that they contain the whole truth, or the only truth." Absorbing such contrasting opinions teaches students to analyze the strength of an argument and compare it to its opposition. From this process readers can inform and strengthen their own opinions, or be exposed to new information that will change their minds. Introducing Issues with Opposing Viewpoints is a mosaic of different voices. The authors are statesmen, pundits, academics, journalists, corporations, and ordinary people who have felt compelled to share their experiences and ideas in a public forum. Their words have been collected from newspapers, journals, books, speeches, interviews, and the Internet, the fastest growing body of opinionated material in the world.

Introducing Issues with Opposing Viewpoints shares many of the well-known features of its critically acclaimed parent series, Opposing Viewpoints. The articles are presented in a pro/con format, allowing readers to absorb divergent perspectives side by side. Active reading questions preface each viewpoint, requiring the student to approach the material thoughtfully and carefully. Useful charts, graphs, and cartoons supplement each article. A thorough introduction provides readers with crucial background on an issue. An annotated bibliography points the reader toward articles, books, and Web sites that contain additional information on the topic. An appendix of organizations to contact contains a wide variety of charities, nonprofit organizations, political groups, and private enterprises that each hold a position on the issue at hand. Finally, a comprehensive index allows readers to locate content quickly and efficiently.

Introducing Issues with Opposing Viewpoints is also significantly different from Opposing Viewpoints. As the series title implies, its presentation will help introduce students to the concept of opposing viewpoints, and learn to use this material to aid in critical writing and debate. The series' four-color, accessible format makes the books attractive and inviting to readers of all levels. In addition, each viewpoint has been carefully edited to maximize a reader's understanding of the content. Short but thorough viewpoints capture the essence of an argument. A substantial, thought-provoking essay question placed at the end of each viewpoint asks the student to further investigate the issues raised in the viewpoint, compare and contrast two authors' arguments, or consider how one might go about forming an opinion on the topic at hand. Each viewpoint contains sidebars that include at-a-glance information and handy statistics. A Facts About section located in the back of the book further supplies students with relevant facts and figures.

Following in the tradition of the Opposing Viewpoints series, Greenhaven Press continues to provide readers with invaluable exposure to the controversial issues that shape our world. As John Stuart Mill once wrote: "The only way in which a human being can make some approach to knowing the whole of a subject is by hearing what can be said about it by persons of every variety of opinion and studying all modes in which it can be looked at by every character of mind. No wise man ever acquired his wisdom in any mode but this." It is to this principle that Introducing Issues with Opposing Viewpoints books are dedicated.

Introduction

Long before the cataclysmic attacks of September 11, 2001, and the wave of changes that followed, a great American warned his fellow citizens about the difficult choices to be made when seeking national security. In 1759 Benjamin Franklin said, "They that can give up essential liberty to obtain a little temporary safety deserve neither liberty nor safety."[1] Deciding what actions might achieve a lasting national security, and whether these compromise the liberty and freedom the United States is famous for, are some of the most critical questions facing lawmakers in the post–September 11 world.

A main tool lawmakers have used in the fight to keep America safe is the Uniting and Strengthening America by Providing Appropriate Tools Required to Intercept and Obstruct Terrorism Act, otherwise known as the Patriot Act. Initially passed immediately after the September 11 attacks and renewed by Congress in 2006, the Patriot Act is a collection of laws that expands authorities' abilities to investigate and prosecute terrorists and other people who would plot to harm Americans.

The Patriot Act was initially passed to help law enforcement agencies catch suspected terrorists. After the September 11 attacks, America learned that the nineteen hijackers who killed nearly three thousand innocent civilians had lived inside the United States, plotting to take American lives as they lived among them. The hijackers had fooled everyone—they lived in ordinary neighborhoods, held jobs, attended schools, had friends, and participated in average American activities like going to bars and restaurants. That the terrorists were able to so thoroughly integrate themselves into American life was frightening, and also revealing. It made authorities realize that if the terrorists could blend in among law-abiding people, they would have to inspect even the most seemingly ordinary citizens in order to catch the terrorists hiding among them.

To this end, the Patriot Act was designed to include provisions such as Section 201, which allows authorities to intercept wire, oral, and electronic communications of citizens; and Section 411, which expands the types of offenses for which immigrants can be deported. A variety of other provisions allow authorities to access private information about

American citizens, such as whether they have ever been members of an organization associated with terrorism. Many argue that the Patriot Act's provisions are not threatening to law-abiding Americans and are good for isolating the activities of terrorists and other people who threaten national security. Public policy analyst Heather Mac Donald has described the Patriot Act as "a balanced updating of surveillance authority in light of the new reality of catastrophic terrorism."[2] Former New York City mayor Edward I. Koch agrees, saying the Patriot Act "is urgently needed in this war against civilized society."[3]

But historically, Americans have fiercely protected themselves against government intrusion in their private lives. Therefore, many people are concerned that portions of the Patriot Act threaten to curb their freedoms for the sake of national security. Indeed, many view it as un-American that seemingly simple—and private—activities such as becoming certified to scuba dive, applying to school, becoming a member of a particular club or group, or checking out a certain type of library book could, under the provisions of the Patriot Act, place a person on a government watch list. "Instead of helping to win the war on terrorism," warns commentator Chuck Baldwin, "the Patriot Act is helping to dismantle fundamental liberties protected by the U.S. Constitution."[4]

Some even argue the Patriot Act offers no additional security at all. People like civil rights attorney Julie Hurwitz say that the Patriot Act does not contain provisions that are useful for thwarting terrorist attacks, only for violating the rights of U.S. citizens. In fact, "there is nothing in the Patriot Act that would have prevented the events of 9/11,"[5] claims Hurwitz. Former Georgia representative Bob Barr agrees. He says that the 9/11 hijackers broke several laws that were already in place at that point to prevent terrorism—for example, they had entered the country illegally, they had fake IDs, and they had illegally learned how to handle aircraft. Even before the Patriot Act, says Barr, "the government had sufficient lawful power to identify and stop the plotters. It failed to do so."[6] Many agree with Hurwitz and Barr that the Patriot Act is just an excuse for authorities to consolidate their power while offering Americans a false sense of security.

Regardless of where people stand on the Patriot Act, most people agree that concern for freedom needs to be balanced with the knowledge that living in a completely open society makes Americans vulnerable to people who wish them harm. If terrorists will seek to blend into American systems, it seems to make sense to put up at least some barriers to prevent them from doing so. Whether the Patriot Act is the appropriate vehicle for this effort, however, remains to be seen. On the one hand, Americans have shown a willingness to surrender a certain level of freedom for security or to tolerate intrusions into their privacy because they feel that being safe is worth it. Indeed, a May 2006 Fox News/Opinion Dynamics poll found that the majority of Americans—54 percent—were willing to give up at least some of their personal freedom if it would reduce the threat of terrorism. Yet at the same time, Americans are split on whether the Patriot Act is a tool that helps the government catch terrorists or one that threatens civil liberties. Also in 2006, a Pew Research Center for the People & the Press survey found that 39 percent of Americans characterized the Patriot Act as a good terrorist-catching law, while 38 percent said it goes too far. Clearly, Americans are still unsure whether the Patriot Act strikes the right balance for their national security needs.

The controversy over the Patriot Act addresses some of the enduring questions about how security and liberty should be balanced in an open society like the United States. These questions are sure to be relevant for a long time to come—just as they were in Benjamin Franklin's time. How best to achieve national security without compromising freedom is at the heart of many of the arguments presented in *Introducing Issues with Opposing Viewpoints: National Security*. Pro/con article pairs expose readers to the basic debates surrounding the quest to achieve national security and encourages them to develop their own opinions on the matter.

Notes
1. Benjamin Franklin, Historical Review of Pennsylvania, 1759.
2. Heather Mac Donald, testimony before the U.S. House of Representatives Committee on the Judiciary, Subcommittee on Crime, Terrorism, and Homeland Security, May 3, 2005. www .manhattan-institute.org/html/mac_donald05-03-05.htm.
3. Edward I. Koch, "The Patriot Act Is Necessary in the Fight Against Terrorism," *Newsmax*, July 27, 2005. http://archive.newsmax.com/ archives/articles/2005/7/26/183338.shtml.

4. Chuck Baldwin, "Patriot Act Is Helping Dismantle Constitutional Liberties," Renewamerica.com, June 13, 2005. www.renewamerica .us/columns/baldwin/050613.

5. Julie Hurwitz, "The PATRIOT Act: Darkness with No Sunset," *Solidarity*, September 2, 2006. www.solidarity-us.org/node/52.

6. Bob Barr, "Patriot Act Games: It Can Happen Here," *American Spectator*, August 19, 2003. www.bobbarr.org/default.asp?pt=news descr&RI=440.

Chapter 1

What Are the Most Serious Threats to National Security?

The possibility of a nuclear attack by terrorists is one of the gravest threats to the United States.

Terrorists Pose a Serious Threat to National Security

Michael Jacobson and Matthew Levitt

"Years after 9/11 we remain in a heightened threat environment."

Terrorists pose a serious threat to U.S. national security, argue Michael Jacobson and Matthew Levitt in the following viewpoint. They explain how the United States has continued to face security breaches even after the terrorist attacks of 9/11, which claimed thousands of American lives. In the authors' opinion, the 9/11 attacks demonstrated how vulnerable the most powerful nation on earth was to a much smaller and more loosely organized enemy. Inspired by America's weakness, hundreds of new terrorist groups began to spring up around the world, and already-existing ones, such as Hezbollah, Hamas, al Qaeda (or al-Qaida), and the Palestinian Islamic Jihad became emboldened in their mission. Consequently, more terrorists now exist than ever before,

Michael Jacobson and Matthew Levitt, "'Franchises' of al-Qaida Pose a Great Threat," *Camden (NJ) Courier-Post*, September 7, 2008. Copyright © 2008 CourierPostOnline.com. All rights reserved. Reproduced by permission.

which increases the likelihood that the United States will be attacked again. For this reason the authors conclude that the authorities need to do everything in their power to guard against a future attack.

Jacobson is a senior fellow in the Washington Institute's Stein Program on Counterterrorism and Intelligence. He previously served as senior adviser in the Office of Terrorism and Financial Intelligence. Levitt is a senior fellow and director of the Stein Program. He also served as deputy assistant secretary for intelligence and analysis at the U.S. Department of the Treasury from 2005 to 2007.

AS YOU READ, CONSIDER THE FOLLOWING QUESTIONS:
1. What terrorist group do the authors say poses the most serious threat to the United States?
2. What three terrorist organizations has al Qaeda partnered with to increase its presence in the Middle East and North Africa, according to Jacobson and Levitt?
3. According to the authors, how many terrorist groups were responsible for terrorist attacks in 2006?

Despite setbacks, al-Qaida remains a potent threat. In mid-August [2008], the U.S. intelligence community's senior ranking terrorism analyst concluded that while increased counterterrorism efforts worldwide have constrained the ability of al-Qaida to attack the United States and its allies, the group "remains the most serious terrorist threat to the United States."

As recently thwarted terrorist plots in Britain, Germany and elsewhere make clear, seven years after 9/11 we remain in a heightened threat environment. But the nature of the transnational threats facing the world today is far different than the ones the United States and its allies faced on 9/11.

The Terrorist Threat Has Multiplied
While al-Qaida itself remains a formidable opponent—particularly with its recent resurgence and secure safe haven in northwest Pakistan—its affiliates and homegrown cells pose a growing threat as

A resurgent al Qaeda in Pakistan has garnered popular support in the country's tribal regions, which has helped al Qaeda reestablish its influence there.

well. As of 9/11, al-Qaida was the main threat facing the United States. At the time of the 9/11 attacks, al-Qaida was a centralized, hierarchical organization directing terrorist operations around the world from its base in Afghanistan.

The United States now faces a different—and in some ways more complicated—threat than it did on 9/11. This is a threat—and an enemy—that continues to evolve rapidly, often in response to U.S. and international pressure. Today [2008], the United States and its allies face a three-fold threat. The first is from the core al-Qaida. While al-Qaida was on its "back foot" from 2004 to 2007, it has now "regained its equilibrium," according to a senior Homeland Security official.

The primary reason for its resurgence is that it has established a de facto safe haven in the tribal areas of Pakistan from which it can direct its global propaganda efforts, and recruit and train terrorist operatives.

Al-Qaida has also successfully expanded its reach through partnerships with other organizations throughout the Middle East and North Africa, described by the State Department's coordinator for counterterrorism, Dell Dailey, as the "franchising of al-Qaida." These affiliates include al-Qaida in Iraq, al-Qaida in the Islamic Maghreb and the Libyan Islamic Fighting Group (LIFG).

Finally, there are more local groups today inspired by al-Qaida, even if they have no direct ties. In fact, there were almost 300 different groups involved in terrorist attacks in 2006—most of them Sunni [the majority sect of Islam]. According to one former intelligence official, more than 40 organizations in all announced formation and pledged allegiance to al-Qaida and Osama bin Laden between January 2005 and April 2007. These groups are located in Syria, Iraq, Lebanon, Europe, Afghanistan, Saudi Arabia, Yemen and Egypt, among others.

Smaller Terrorist Groups Are Harder to Fight

The shift in the terrorist threat is largely attributable to U.S. and international efforts after 9/11 to crack down on al-Qaida. With tighter border security, document control and financial tracking, al-Qaida recognized that it would be more effective if it used local groups to conduct its attacks. While the al-Qaida core is somewhat resurgent, it is still a far more decentralized model than the al-Qaida of 9/11.

Most Experts Think Another Terrorist Attack Is Likely

A survey of more than one hundred top foreign policy experts revealed that the majority think the United States will experience another terrorist attack on the scale of 9/11 within ten years. Even more likely, in their opinion, is a smaller-scale attack that targets a subway, bus, or train.

Question: What is the likelihood of a terrorist attack on the scale of the 9/11 attacks occurring again in the United States in the following time frames?

	No chance/ Unlikely	Likely/ Certain
Within 6 months......................	76	24
Within 5 years.........................	37	63
Within 10 years......................	29	71

Question: Now consider the subway attacks that took place in London in July 2005 and the train attacks in Madrid in March 2004. What is the likelihood of a terrorist attack on this scale occurring in the United States in the following time frames?

	No chance/ Unlikely	Likely/ Certain
Within 6 months......................	62	38
Within 5 years.........................	17	83
Within 10 years......................	15	85

Taken from: *Foreign Policy*, "The Terrorism Index," May 2008.

Although al-Qaida and its affiliates may still present the most serious threat to the U.S., focusing on this group alone would be a mistake. Groups such as Hezbollah, PKK [Kurdistan Workers Party], Hamas and Palestinian Islamic Jihad remain terrorist threats, focused not only on their operations at home but also on maintaining their financial and logistical support networks internationally. And, even more disturbing, as Rolf Mowatt-Larssen, the [U.S.] Department of Energy's intelligence chief warns, "the threat posed by nuclear terrorism is much broader than the aspirations of any single terrorist group."

Strategic Efforts Are Needed to Beat Terrorists

To be sure, counterterrorism will remain a top national security priority for [President Barack Obama's administration]. Ongoing tactical efforts to capture and kill hardened terrorists, however, need to be better combined with strategic efforts to counter the increasing radicalization of disaffected Muslim youth (particularly in Europe) and to highlight al-Qaida's bankrupt ideology and contest its violent and intolerant message.

We will not be able to say we are defeating al-Qaida and its allies until we are effectively countering their message and narrative, and beating them not only on the physical battlefield, but in the virtual ones as well.

EVALUATING THE AUTHORS' ARGUMENTS:

Michael Jacobson and Matthew Levitt argue that al Qaeda has expanded its reach around the world by "franchising" itself. Clarify what the authors mean by this. Do you think these terrorist franchises have increased America's chance of being attacked by terrorists in the future? Explain your answer thoroughly.

The National Security Threat from Terrorism Has Been Exaggerated

"Though al Qaeda may— emphasize 'may'—still have the capacity to mount the occasional major operation, that doesn't mean terrorism should be treated as an omnipresent, existential threat."

Steve Chapman

In the following viewpoint Steve Chapman argues that the threat from terrorism has been exaggerated. While horrific terrorist attacks do occur, Chapman contends they are rare and isolated events. He says most terrorists are "amateurs" and do not have the resources, skills, or know-how to launch serious attacks on America or its allies. Furthermore, in terms of the threat to human life, terrorists kill very few people as compared to outright war. Despite these facts, the fear of a future terrorist attack is deeply embedded in the American psyche. Chapman concludes that the United States is not likely to face another attack on the scale of 9/11 and that the U.S. government should redirect its foreign policies to other national security concerns.

Chapman is a columnist and editorial writer for the *Chicago Tribune*. He is also a frequent contributor to *Reason*, a monthly magazine that covers politics and culture for "free minds and free markets."

AS YOU READ, CONSIDER THE FOLLOWING QUESTIONS:
1. How many terrorist attacks does Chapman say have taken place on U.S. soil since September 11, 2001?
2. According to Chapman, how many people do terrorists kill outside of war zones worldwide each year?
3. How many Americans does the author say were murdered each year when violent crime was at its peak, compared to the number killed by terrorists?

For anyone who has grown complacent about the danger of terrorism, the [2007] incidents in London [England] and Glasgow[1] [Scotland] were supposed to provide a jolt of reality. As former federal prosecutor Andrew McCarthy put it, "these foiled attacks are best understood as new rounds in a long, global war, provoked by the challenge of radical Islam." Here was proof that the jihadists are still out there, ready to strike at the moment of their choosing.

Homeland Security Secretary Michael Chertoff clearly agrees. On a visit Tuesday [July 10, 2007] to the *Chicago Tribune*, he said he has a "gut feeling" an attack may be imminent. "The intent to attack us remains as strong as it was on Sept. 10, 2001," he declared.

Well, no one in that job is ever going to say the danger has been overstated. But the truth is that intent and ability are not the same thing. Though al Qaeda may—emphasize "may"—still have the capacity to mount the occasional major operation, that doesn't mean terrorism should be treated as an omnipresent, existential threat.

Most Terrorists Are Amateurs
In reality, this fight bears only a faint resemblance to a real war. Only rarely can al Qaeda and its imitators manage a strike against their prime enemies, Britain and the United States, and even more rarely

1. The incidents referred to involve unexploded car bombs found in London's Theatre District and an SUV that rammed into the Glasgow International Airport.

As evidence that the international terrorist threat is overstated, the author points out that many terrorists, like those alleged to have planted unexploded car bombs in the United Kingdom, are unskilled amateurs.

can they succeed. Like the alleged terrorists who planned to attack Fort Dix and JFK International Airport, the perpetrators in Britain were not trained professionals but bumbling amateurs.

On Sept. 12, 2001, it was easy to believe that we would suffer dozens of major attacks on U.S. soil over the next six years, and almost impossible to imagine we would suffer none. Instead of being the opening blitz of a "long, global war," 9/11 was a freak event that may never be replicated.

In a real war, such as the ones we are fighting in Iraq and Afghanistan, many people die, week in and week out. But John Mueller, a national security professor at Ohio State University, notes that in a typical year, no more than a few hundred people are killed worldwide in attacks by al Qaeda and similar groups outside of war zones.

That's too many, but it's not a danger on the order of Nazi Germany or the Soviet Union or even Saddam Hussein. It's more like organized crime—an ongoing problem demanding unceasing vigilance, a malady that can be contained but never eliminated.

False Alarms in the U.S. War on Terror

Earlier in the war on terror, authorities frequently issued threat warnings—yet all of these were proven to be exaggerated or unfounded.

Date	The Threat	The Reality
Sept. 10, 2002	President George W. Bush announces the nation's first "orange alert"; Vice President Dick Cheney goes to a "secure location."	No specific threat was made against an American target.
May 20, 2003	United States is placed on orange alert after a warning that al Qaeda has entered an operational period.	No specific threat is ever cited.
July 29, 2003	Dept. of Homeland Security warns that new 9/11-like strikes are in the works and predicts at least one will be executed over the summer.	None of the alleged attacks ever materialized.
May 26, 2004	Attorney General John Ashcroft warns that an al Qaeda plot is "90 percent" arranged.	The threat Ashcroft spoke of came from a discredited group that is not taken seriously by Western intelligence agencies.
June 14, 2004	An Ohio shopping mall is said to be threatened by an al Qaeda bomber.	It is revealed the suspected bomber had been in custody for seven months on charges that had nothing to do with a shopping mall.
August 1, 2004	An orange alert is issued as the result of a threat against the Citigroup Building and the New York Stock Exchange.	Reports reveal the intelligence is three years old.
October 6, 2004	The FBI warns that al Qaeda will bomb the New York subway system on or around October 9. President George W. Bush claims to have foiled ten terrorist plots since 9/11.	The subway bombing warning is reported by officials to be unfounded. All of the plots Bush claimed to have foiled are revealed to have been nonoperational.

Compiled by book editor from *Rolling Stone*, "The Phony War," September 11, 2006.

U.S. Security Policies Threaten Americans

By framing the fight as a global war, we have helped Osama bin Laden and hurt ourselves. Had we treated him and his confederates as the moral equivalent of international drug lords or sex traffickers, the organization might not have the romantic image it has acquired. By exaggerating the potential impact, we also magnified the disruptive effect of any plots, which is just what the terrorists seek.

We do further harm to ourselves by accepting government actions we would never tolerate except in the context of war. Recently, a federal appeals court threw out a lawsuit challenging the National Security Agency's secret surveillance of phone calls made between the United States and foreign countries.

The judges' reasoning was right out of "Catch-22":[2] You can't sue unless you can prove you've been wiretapped, but you can't prove it because the wiretappers won't tell you. The government abuses its power secretly, in the name of national security, and the secrecy protects it from having to end the abuse.

> ## FAST FACT
>
> The Crisis in the Middle East Task Force reports that very few people outside of war zones are killed by "Muslim extremists" each year. In fact, more people drown in bathtubs each year in the United States.

Crime is a serious national problem that used to be even worse. At the height of the mayhem, more than 24,000 Americans were murdered annually—a Sept. 11, 2001, attack every six weeks. Yet even when the toll was at its worst, we insisted that police respect the constitutional rights of suspected criminals. We maintained the limits on the power of the president and other law enforcement officials to investigate and imprison people. For the most part, we kept our perspective.

An Exaggerated Threat Hurts Civil Liberties

After the World Trade Center came down, by contrast, we let ourselves be convinced that many restrictions were an unaffordable lux-

---

2. A satirical historical novel by American author Joseph Heller. The phrase refers to a "no-win situation."

ury. Any concern for civil liberties was met with the retort: "We're at war." And in war, anything goes.

The 9/11 attack was a crisis that has largely passed, but no one in Washington wants to admit it. It's politically safer to depict the danger as undiminished no matter how long we go without an attack. But someday, we will look back and ask if we were acting out of sensible caution or unfounded panic.

EVALUATING THE AUTHORS' ARGUMENTS:

In this viewpoint Steve Chapman considers most terrorists to be nothing more than amateur members of an organized crime family. The authors of the preceding viewpoint, Michael Jacobson and Matthew Levitt, on the other hand, argue that terrorist organizations are replicating at a staggering speed and pose a serious and imminent danger to the United States. With which perspective do you agree? Why?

America's Foreign Oil Dependence Is a Threat to National Security

David Sandalow

"Because we depend so completely on oil . . . we empower oil-exporting nations that wish us ill."

In the following viewpoint David Sandalow argues that America's national security is threatened by its dependence on foreign oil. America relies heavily on foreign oil imports from the Persian Gulf to meet its energy needs. Sandalow claims this dependence has forced the United States to get involved in several conflicts in the Middle East, including the Persian Gulf War in 1991 and the current war in Iraq. As a result, many Middle Eastern nations and terrorist groups have become strongly anti-American, harboring deep resentment toward America's presence in the region and its meddling in regional affairs. This hatred, says Sandalow, is what fuels terrorism. Further adding to the problem is the fact that terrorist organizations are often financed by money earned

David Sandalow, "Ending Oil Dependence: Protecting National Security, the Environment, and the Economy," *Opportunity 08: Independent Ideas for America's Next President*, edited by Michael E. O'Hanlon, Brookings Institution, 2008, p. 3. Copyright © 2007 The Brookings Institution. Reproduced by permission.

from oil exports. In this sense, says Sandalow, America's oil money is funding the very terrorist groups that threaten it. Sandalow concludes that America must reduce its foreign oil consumption and look to alternative energy sources if it wants to protect itself from future terrorist attacks.

Sandalow is an energy and environment scholar at the Brookings Institution, an independent research and policy institute. He was also a senior staff director of the National Security Council during President Bill Clinton's administration.

AS YOU READ, CONSIDER THE FOLLOWING QUESTIONS:
1. In what year does the author say the United States expelled Saddam Hussein from the oil-rich nation of Kuwait?
2. Oil money from what Middle Eastern nation fuels anti-American views among terrorists, according to Sandalow?
3. According to the author, what oil-exporting nation poses the largest threat to U.S. national security?

Large majorities of Americans agree that oil dependence is a serious problem. National security hawks raise alarms about vast sums sent to the Persian Gulf. Environmentalists warn about global warming. Farmers see new fortunes in a transition to ethanol. Consumers cry out when oil prices rise. Politicians as different as President George W. Bush, Senator Richard Lugar (R-Ind.), Senator Tom Harkin (D-Iowa), and Democratic National Committee Chair Howard Dean all call for an end to Americans' oil "addiction."

Yet today oil provides more than 97 percent of the fuel for our vehicles, barely different than a generation ago. Oil use continues to climb, in the United States and around the world. Meanwhile game-changing technologies are moving closer to market, propelled by considerable investor interest. Plug-in hybrid engines and biofuels could reshape the transportation sector. In the years ahead, a confluence of factors—political, technological, and financial—will create an opportunity for transformational change. With sustained commitment, the [new] President can help end the United States' debilitating dependence on oil.

The Oil Paradox

First, a question: How did a product so widely used become so widely resented? Oil is a high-energy-content, easily transportable fuel. Trillions of dollars of infrastructure is already in place to convert it into services people want around the world.

Oddly perhaps, this extraordinary success lies at the heart of the problem. Oil's dominance as a transportation fuel is so total, it shapes relations among nation-states. Oil's reward is so rich, it shapes entire economies. Oil's emissions are growing so rapidly, they are warming the planet.

Call it the Oil Paradox. Oil's enormous success creates epic problems. Because we depend so completely on oil, we devote extraordinary political and military resources to securing it, at staggering cost. We empower oil-exporting nations that wish us ill. . . .

Desire for Oil Breeds Terrorism

The United States is in a long war. Islamic fundamentalists struck our shores and are determined to do so again. *Oil dependence is an important cause of this threat.* For example, according to Brent Scowcroft, National Security Adviser at the time of the first Gulf War, ". . . what gave enormous urgency to [Iraqi dictator Saddam Hussein's invasion of Kuwait] was the issue of oil." After removing Saddam from Kuwait in 1991, U.S. troops remained in Saudi Arabia where their presence bred great resentment. Osama bin Laden's first fatwa [religious decree], in 1996, was titled "Declaration of War against the Americans Occupying the Land of the Two Holy Places."

FAST FACT

Sixty-seven percent of the American public said that decreasing America's dependence on Middle East oil is "a very important step in preventing terrorism," according to a 2006 poll by the Pew Research Center.

Today [2008], deep resentment of the U.S. role in the Persian Gulf is a powerful *jihadist* [Islamic religious warrior] recruitment tool. Resentment grows not just from the war in Iraq, but also from our relationship with the House of Saud, the presence of our forces throughout

America's massive military presence in the oil-rich Persian Gulf has proved a powerful recruitment tool for jihadists.

the region, and more. Yet the United States cannot easily extricate itself from this contentious region. The Persian Gulf has half the world's proven oil reserves, the world's cheapest oil, and its only spare production capacity. So long as modern vehicles run only on oil, the Persian Gulf will remain an indispensable region for the global economy.

Oil Money Is Used to Finance Terrorists

Furthermore, *the huge flow of oil money into the region helps finance terrorist networks.* Saudi money provides critical support for *madrassas*[1] promulgating virulent anti-American views. Still worse, diplomatic efforts to enlist Saudi government help in choking off such funding, or even to investigate terrorist attacks, are hampered by the

---

1. Islamic religious schools.

The United States Is Dependent on Foreign Oil

According to the Natural Resources Defense Council, the United States spends more than $200,000 per minute on foreign oil. Sending so much money overseas is believed to undermine America's national security.

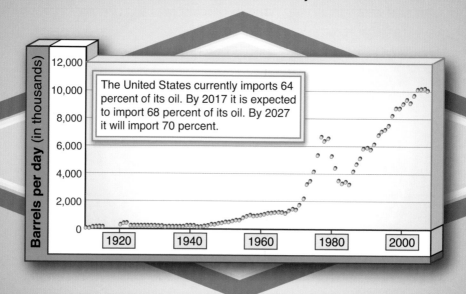

> The United States currently imports 64 percent of its oil. By 2017 it is expected to import 68 percent of its oil. By 2027 it will import 70 percent.

Taken from: U.S. Energy Information Administration, 2009.

priority we attach to preserving Saudi cooperation in managing world oil markets.

Held Hostage by Our Oil Dependence

This points to a broader problem—*oil dependence reduces the world community's leverage in responding to threats from oil-exporting nations.* Today, the most prominent threat comes from Iran, whose nuclear ambitions could further destabilize the Persian Gulf and put powerful new weapons into the hands of terrorists. Yet efforts to respond to this threat with multilateral sanctions have foundered on fears that Iran would retaliate by withholding oil from world markets. In short, three decades after the first oil shocks—and a quarter-century after the humiliating capture of U.S. diplomats in Tehran—we remain hostage to our continuing dependence on oil.

Americans' Safety Threatened by Oil Dependence

Finally, *oil dependence jeopardizes the safety of our men and women in uniform.* Fuel convoys are highly vulnerable to ambush. Diesel generators display an easily detected heat signature. In many Army deployments, oil makes up a staggering 70 percent of the tonnage that must be transported to the front lines. In June 2006, Major General Richard Zilmer, head of the Multi-National Force in Al-Anbar Province, Iraq, made a "Priority 1" request for renewable energy technologies on the front lines. Zilmer's memo declared that, without renewable power, U.S. forces "will remain unnecessarily exposed" and will "continue to accrue preventable . . . serious and grave casualties." . . .

Foreign Oil Policy Must Change

Traditional oil diplomacy focuses on securing adequate and reliable supplies. This will remain a necessary element of U.S. diplomacy for years to come. But this strategy must be supplemented by another: reducing oil dependence in all consuming nations.

Oil is a fungible product, traded globally. Improvements in fuel efficiency and the use of clean alternative fuels benefit the United States wherever they occur. Improving fuel efficiency in China could do more to protect our national security, fight global warming, and promote economic growth than securing additional supply from the Persian Gulf. (Improving fuel efficiency in the United States could be even better.) To speed the diffusion of oil-saving technologies and promote rapid transformation of global transportation fleets, the [new] President [Barack Obama] should give priority to cooperative dialogues that encourage, for example, global adoption of plug-in hybrid engines and sustainable production of biofuels. . . .

The United States Must Address Security Challenges

Ending oil dependence doesn't mean ending oil use. It means ending our near-total reliance on oil as a transportation fuel. It means giving drivers a choice between oil and other fuels. . . .

The problem of oil dependence cannot be solved by tinkering at the margins. An unusual political consensus and game-changing technologies give . . . President [Obama] a rare opportunity to address several of the nation's most important security, environmental and economic challenges.

EVALUATING THE AUTHOR'S ARGUMENTS:

In this viewpoint Sandalow argues that America's dependence on foreign oil poses a serious national security risk. What pieces of evidence does he provide to support his claim? Did he convince you of his argument? Explain why or why not.

America's Foreign Oil Dependence Is Not a Threat to National Security

Jerry Taylor and Peter Van Doren

"Cutting back on oil consumption would most likely not cut back on terrorism."

In the following viewpoint Jerry Taylor and Peter Van Doren argue that America's national security is not threatened by its dependence on foreign oil. They admit that America imports a lot of its oil from the Persian Gulf, but they argue that the money from that oil does not end up in the hands of terrorists. Oil proceeds are not paid directly to terrorists, and the authors believe terrorists rarely see a portion of these proceeds. Furthermore, if terrorists really wanted to attack the United States, they would not need oil money to do it. Most terrorist attacks are pulled off on very small budgets with inexpensive materials. Finally, most terrorist groups are funded by non-oil-exporting countries, which casts further doubt on the

Jerry Taylor and Peter Van Doren, "Driving Bin Laden? Oil Consumption Has Little to Do with Terrorism," NationalReview.com, March 8, 2006. Copyright © National Review Online, 2006. All Rights Reserved. Reproduced by permission.

oil-terrorism connection. The authors believe that *less* oil money in the Middle East could actually cause terrorism—the oil industry employs many Middle Easterners, who the authors think might be sympathetic to terrorist groups if they suddenly became unemployed. Overall, the authors believe the relationship between oil dependence and terrorism is weak and poses no serious threat to America's national security.

Taylor and Van Doren are senior fellows at the Cato Institute, a nonprofit public policy research foundation. Van Doren is also the editor of *Regulation*, the Cato Institute's quarterly magazine that examines regulatory policies.

AS YOU READ, CONSIDER THE FOLLOWING QUESTIONS:
1. According to Taylor and Van Doren, how much did it cost to execute the 9/11 attacks?
2. What three non-oil-rich nations do the authors say provided the most money to Islamic terrorists during the 1990s?
3. What is the most important thing terrorist organizations require to function, according to the authors?

When you drive alone, do you drive with [al Qaeda leader Osama] bin Laden? A growing number of foreign policy analysts seem to think so, and the president [George W. Bush] himself said as much in an interview with CBS News anchor Bob Schieffer a few days before his much-ballyhooed "State of the Addiction" speech to a joint session of Congress. Unfortunately, the widespread belief that conservation and alternative fuels will cripple Islamic terrorism is wishful thinking.

Terrorists Do Not Need Oil Money
The fundamental problem with the argument is that terrorists don't need oil revenues. The fact that catastrophic terrorism can be undertaken on the proverbial dime (a few hundred thousand dollars paid for the 9/11 attacks) suggests that choking off financial resources to al Qaeda effectively is a hopeless task.

Further evidence of the unimportance of money to terrorism is the absence of a correlation between Persian Gulf oil revenues and terrorist activity. Oil prices and profits during the 1990s were among the lowest ever seen in history. But the 1990s also witnessed the worldwide spread of Wahabbi fundamentalism and the coming of age of al Qaeda. Note too that Islamic terrorists in the 1990s relied upon help from state sponsors such as Sudan, Afghanistan, and Pakistan—nations that aren't exactly known for their oil wealth or robust economies.

Less Oil Money Creates More Terrorists

So terrorists don't rely on oil revenues. What terrorists need most is a recruiting pool from which to draw. Question: how do you suppose the Muslim world would react to a U.S. policy that had the stated intention of impoverishing Muslims in suspect parts of the world? Lower oil profits, after all, mean smaller state payments to young, underemployed Muslims and a less robust economy.

To the extent that deteriorating economic conditions breed social discontent and political resentment (which could easily be blamed on the United States), "starving the oil beast" might well increase the recruitment pool for al Qaeda and invite producer states to reconsider their allegiances in the war on terror. Even though our purchase of oil from some countries does prop up some truly pathological regimes, cutting back on oil consumption might produce even more pathological regimes.

> **FAST FACT**
>
> America does not import most of its oil from the Middle East and terrorist-supporting nations. As of February 2009, America imported 37 percent of its oil from Canada and Mexico, according to the Energy Information Administration.

Most Oil States Do Not Fund Terrorism

Reducing oil revenue to noxious regimes? This might be a risk worth taking if billions were finding their way from such regimes into al Qaeda coffers, but that seems unlikely. Everything we know suggests that al Qaeda terrorist cells are "pay as you go" operations that primarily engage

The authors argue that although oil-rich states are funding madrassas, like the one shown here, it is actually the oil-poor states like Afghanistan that are funding al Qaeda.

in garden-variety crime to fund their activities. Given that the governments of Saudi Arabia, Kuwait, and others in the region are slated for extinction should bin Laden have his way, those governments have no interest in facilitating the transfer of oil revenues to some post office box in Pakistan.

Producer states do use oil revenues to fund ideological extremism, and Saudi financing of madrassas[1] is the primary case in point. But given the importance of that undertaking to the Saudi government (it was instituted, after all, to defend the House of Saud's position of leadership in the Islamic world in response to criticism from radical Shiites from Iran), it's unlikely that the Saudis would cease and desist simply because profits were down. They certainly weren't deterred by meager oil profits in the 1990s.

The United States Should Not Provide Security for Oil-Producing Countries

So cutting back on oil consumption would most likely not cut back on terrorism. But wouldn't a cutback reduce the need for a military presence in the Persian Gulf? No, because there is no need for a U.S. military presence in the Gulf regardless of the amount of oil we import.

It's certainly true that a disruption of the oil supply from the Middle East would increase the price of crude oil everywhere in the world.

1. Islamic religious schools.

The Top Fifteen Sources of Crude Oil Imported by the United States

At the end of 2008, two of the top three nations exporting oil to the United States were Canada and Mexico, which have no connection to terrorism. Experts say importing foreign oil is not a problem when it comes from friendly sources like these.

Country	Barrels of Oil per Day (1,000s) December 2008
Canada	2,033
Saudi Arabia	1,394
Mexico	1,126
Venezuela	1,028
Nigeria	869
Angola	553
Iraq	519
Ecuador	252
Algeria	235
Brazil	208
Kuwait	194
Colombia	148
Chad	105
Congo (Brazzaville)	95
Azerbaijan	78

Taken from: Energy Information Administration, 2009.

But just because the security of Middle Eastern oil has the characteristics of a public good for all consumers in the world does not imply that the United States has to provide that security. Oil producers will provide for their own security needs as long as the cost of doing so is less than the profit they gain from the oil trade. Given that their economies are so heavily dependent upon oil revenues, they have even more incentive than we do to worry about the security of production facilities, ports, and sea lanes. And if producing countries provide inadequate security in the eyes of consuming countries, consuming countries can pay producers to augment it.

In short, whatever security our presence provides (and many analysts think that our presence actually reduces security) could be provided by other parties were the U.S. to withdraw. The fact that Saudi Arabia and Kuwait paid for 55 percent of the cost of Operation Desert Storm suggests that keeping the [Straits] of Hormuz free of trouble is certainly within their means. The same argument applies to al Qaeda threats to oil production facilities.

The Relationship Between Oil and Terrorism Is Weak

It's no surprise that the political class has convinced itself that bigger handouts to farmers and more automobile regulation constitute a "secret weapon" in the war against bin Laden. It is a surprise, however, that so many otherwise serious people are willing to believe them.

EVALUATING THE AUTHORS' ARGUMENTS:

Taylor and Van Doren argue that America's reliance on foreign oil does not breed terrorism. And yet, many terrorist groups are based in the Middle East, one of the largest oil-producing regions in the world. How do you make sense of this discrepancy? In your opinion, do you think there is any connection between oil and terrorism? Explain why or why not.

Climate Change Is a Threat to National Security

"Climate change has the potential to disrupt our way of life and force changes in how we keep ourselves safe and secure."

CNA Corporation

The Military Advisory Board of the CNA Corporation argues in the following viewpoint, taken from a 2007 climate change study, that climate change is a serious threat to national security. The board explains that climate change is expected to result in extreme weather events, such as drought, flooding, hurricanes, and rising sea levels. These disasters will cause habitat changes, decreased food supply, water shortages, and higher rates of disease, all of which will cause chaos, instability, and conflict on a global scale. For these reasons, the board concludes that climate change should be regarded as a national security threat.

The CNA Corporation is a nonprofit institution that conducts independent research and analysis on a wide array of public interest concerns. The Military Advisory Board convened for this climate change study included twelve retired U.S. admirals and generals.

AS YOU READ, CONSIDER THE FOLLOWING QUESTIONS:
1. According to the authors, by 2025 what percent of the world's population will live in countries where there is too little water?
2. What do the authors say furthered, or exacerbated, the Rwandan genocide of 1994?
3. A three-foot rise in sea level could submerge what four areas of the United States, according to the authors?

One reason human civilizations have grown and flourished over the last five millennia is that the world's climate has been relatively stable. However, when climates change significantly or environmental conditions deteriorate to the point that necessary resources are not available, societies can become stressed, sometimes to the point of collapse.

For those concerned about national security, stability is a primary goal. Maintaining stability within and among nations is often a means of avoiding full-scale military conflicts. Conversely, instability in key areas can threaten our security. For these reasons, a great deal of our national security efforts in the post–World War II era have been focused on protecting stability where it exists and trying to instill it where it does not.

This brings us to the connection between climate change and national security.

Climate Change Causes Instability

As noted, climate change involves much more than temperature increases. It can bring with it many of the kinds of changes in natural systems that have introduced instability among nations throughout the centuries. . . .

For example:

- Some nations may have impaired access to food and water.
- Violent weather, and perhaps land loss due to rising sea levels and increased storm surges, can damage infrastructure and uproot large numbers of people.
- These changes, and others, may create large numbers of migrants. When people cross borders in search of resources, tensions can arise.

The Threat from Climate Change

Many countries, including the United States, have millions of residents who live in low-lying coastal areas. If climate change causes seas to rise and coastal areas to flood (as experts expect), tens of millions of people will be left homeless and contribute to chaos and instability.

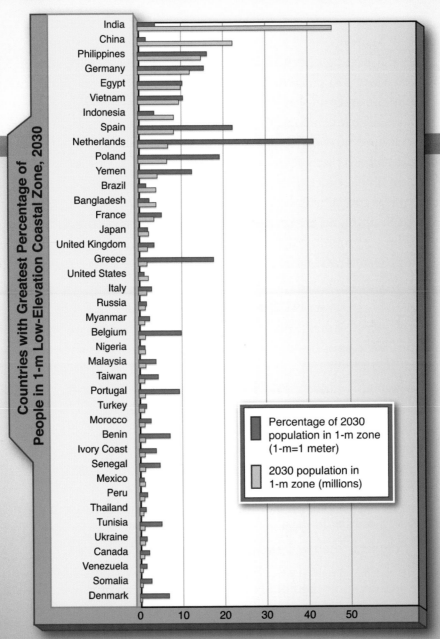

Taken from: Center for Earth Science Information Network, "Assessment of Select Climate Change Impacts on U.S. National Security," Columbia University, July 1, 2008.

- Many governments, even some that look stable today, may be unable to deal with these new stresses. When governments are ineffective, extremism can gain a foothold.
- While the developed world will be far better equipped to deal with the effects of climate change, some of the poorest regions may be affected most. This gap can potentially provide an avenue for extremist ideologies and create the conditions for terrorism. . . .

Failed States Can Lead to Terrorism

Many developing countries do not have the government and social infrastructures in place to cope with the types of stressors that could be brought on by global climate change.

When a government can no longer deliver services to its people, ensure domestic order, and protect the nation's borders from invasion, conditions are ripe for turmoil, extremism and terrorism to fill the vacuum. Lebanon's experience with the terrorist group Hezbollah and the Brazilian government's attempts to rein in the slum gang First Capital Command are both examples of how the central governments' inability to provide basic services has led to strengthening of these extra-governmental entities.

Mass Migrations Add to Global Tensions

The reasons for mass migrations are very complex. However, when water or food supplies shift or when conditions otherwise deteriorate (as from sea level rise, for example), people will likely move to find more favorable conditions. Although climate change may force migrations of workers due to economic conditions, the greatest concern will be movement of asylum seekers and refugees who due to ecological devastation become settlers:

- By 2025, 40 percent of the world's population will be living in countries experiencing significant water shortages.
- Over the course of this century, sea level rise could potentially cause the displacement of tens of millions of people from low-lying areas such as Bangladesh.

Migrations in themselves do not necessarily have negative effects, although taken in the context of global climate change a net benefit is highly unlikely. Three types of migration patterns occur.

Some migrations take place within countries, adding to a nation's political stress, causing economic upheaval—positive and negative—and distracting from other issues. As a developed nation, the U.S. was able to absorb the displacement of people from the Gulf Coast in the wake of Hurricane Katrina without suffering economic or political collapse, but not without considerable turmoil.

Some migrations cross international borders. Environmental degradation can fuel migrations in less developed countries, and these migrations can lead to international political conflict. For example, the large migration from Bangladesh to India in the second half of the last century was due largely to loss of arable land, among other environmental factors. This affected the economy and political situation in the regions of India that absorbed most of this population shift and resulted in violence between natives and migrants.

A third form of migration involves not only crossing international borders but moving across vast regions while doing so. Since the 1960s, Europe has experienced this kind of "south to north" migration, with an influx of immigrants from Africa and Asia. The shift in demographics has created racial and religious tensions in many European countries, as evidenced in the 2005 civil unrest in France.

> **FAST FACT**
>
> The deputy director of National Intelligence for Analysis says that sixty-three U.S. coastal military installations and a number of nuclear reactors are in danger of being flooded by storm surges caused by global warming.

Resource Scarcity Leads to Conflict

To live in stability, human societies need access to certain fundamental resources, the most important of which are water and food. The lack, or mismanagement, of these resources can undercut the stability of local populations; it can affect regions on a national or international scale.

Disputes over key resources such as water do not automatically trigger violent outcomes, and no recent wars have been waged solely over water resources. In areas with a strong government and societal cohesiveness, even tense disputes and resource crises can be peacefully overcome. In fact, in recent years, arguments have been made that multinational cooperation over precious water resources has been more an instrument of regional peace than of war.

Nevertheless, resource scarcity always has the potential to be a contributing factor to conflict and instability in areas with weak and weakly supported governments. In addition, there is always the potential for regional fighting to spread to a national or international scale. Some recent examples include: the 1994 genocide in Rwanda that was furthered by violence over agricultural resources; the situation in Darfur, Sudan, which had land resources at its root and which is increasingly spilling over into neighboring Chad; the 1970s downfall of Ethiopian Emperor Haile Selassie through his government's inability to respond to food shortages; and the 1974 Nigerian coup that resulted largely from an insufficient response to famine.

Whether resource scarcity proves to be the impetus for peaceful cooperation or an instigator of conflict in the future remains to be seen. Regions that are already water scarce (such as Kuwait, Jordan, Israel, Rwanda, Somalia, Algeria, and Kenya) may be forced to confront this choice as climate change exacerbates their water scarcity. . . .

U.S. Water Sources Are Threatened by Climate Change

The primary security threats to the U.S. arise from the potential demand for humanitarian aid and a likely increase in immigration from neighbor states. It is important to remember that the U.S. will be dealing with its own climate change issues at the same time. . . .

Drought and decreased rainfall is projected to . . . affect the central southern U.S. That could have significant impact on food production and sources of water for millions. The High Plains (or "Ogallala") aquifer underlies much of the semi-arid west-central U.S. The aquifer provides water for 27 percent of the irrigated land in the country and supplies about 30 percent of the groundwater used for irrigation. In fact, three of the top grain-producing states—Texas, Kansas, and Nebraska—each get 70 to 90 percent of their irrigation water from the Ogallala aquifer. Human-induced stresses on this groundwater have resulted in water-table declines greater than 100 feet in some areas. This already difficult situation could be greatly exacerbated by a decrease in rainfall predicted for the region. Similarly, a recent study by the National Research Council on the Colorado River basin (the river is the main water source for tens of millions of people in the Southwest) predicted substantial decreases in river flow, based on higher population coupled with the climate change effects. . . .

Increased Natural Disasters Are Likely

Flooding could increase with sea level rises, especially in the low-lying areas of North America—inundation models from the University of Arizona project that a sea level rise of three feet would cause much of Miami, Fort Myers, a large portion of the Everglades, and all of the Florida Keys to disappear.

In the past, U.S. military forces have responded to natural disasters, and are likely to continue doing so in the foreseeable future. The

This graphic shows areas in the United States that would be affected by a one-meter rise in sea levels. Millions of Americans would be affected.

ea level
e could
shape
e nation

bal warming –
·ugh a combination
1elting glaciers,
appearing ice
·ets and warmer
·ers expanding –
·ld cause oceans to
· by one meter, or
·ut 39 inches.

■ **Area affected by**
a 1-meter sea rise

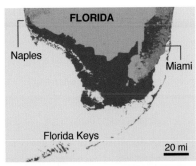

CE: University of Arizona

military was deployed to Central America after Hurricane Mitch in 1998 and to Haiti following the rains and mudslides of 2004. The U.S. military was also heavily involved in the response to Hurricane Katrina. Climate change will likely increase calls for this type of mission in the Americas in the future.

U.S. Migration Will Increase

The greater problem for the U.S. may be an increased flow of migrants northward into the U.S. Already, a large volume of south to north migration in the Americas is straining some states and is the subject of national debate. The migration is now largely driven by economics and political instability. The rate of immigration from Mexico to the U.S. is likely to rise because the water situation in Mexico is already marginal and could worsen with less rainfall and more droughts. Increases in weather disasters, such as hurricanes elsewhere, will also stimulate migrations to the U.S. . . .

Climate Change Could Disrupt America's Way of Life

Potential threats to the nation's security require careful study and prudent planning—to counter and mitigate potential detrimental outcomes. Based on the evidence presented, the Military Advisory Board concluded that it is appropriate to focus on the serious consequences to our national security that are likely from unmitigated climate change. In already-weakened states, extreme weather events, drought, flooding, sea level rise, retreating glaciers, and the rapid spread of life-threatening diseases will themselves have likely effects: increased migrations, further weakened and failed states, expanded ungoverned spaces, exacerbated underlying conditions that terrorist groups seek to exploit, and increased internal conflicts. In developed countries, these conditions threaten to disrupt economic trade and introduce new security challenges, such as increased spread of infectious disease and increased immigration.

Overall, climate change has the potential to disrupt our way of life and force changes in how we keep ourselves safe and secure by adding a new hostile and stressing factor into the national and international security environment.

EVALUATING THE AUTHORS' ARGUMENTS:

In the viewpoint you just read, the Military Advisory Board of the CNA Corporation uses history, facts, and examples to make the argument that climate change poses a serious threat to U.S. national security. The authors do not, however, use any quotations to support their points. If you were to rewrite the article and insert quotations, what authorities might you quote from? Where would you place these quotations to bolster the points the authors make?

Climate Change Is Not a Threat to National Security

George Neumayr

> *"If a threat to the future of civilization exists, it will come not from the environment but from environmentalists."*

In the following viewpoint George Neumayr argues that climate change does not pose a threat to America's national security. This is because, in his opinion, catastrophic global warming—that is, global warming significant enough to cause widespread disaster—does not even exist. He says politicians who warn about the security implications of global warming are creating alarmism, or mass hysteria, among the American people. Neumayr warns that such alarmism will lead to poor global warming policies that will ultimately hurt American businesses. He concludes that environmentalists pose a far greater threat to the nation than does global warming.

Neumayr is editor of *Catholic World Report* and a press critic for the *California Political Review*.

Protecting the country from non-existent threats while exposing it to real ones is likely to define the incoming administration. So it is appropriate that Hillary Clinton, in her opening remarks before the Senate on Tuesday, identified as an "unambiguous security threat" something that doesn't even exist — catastrophic global warming.

Although some experts contend that pollution—such as smoke seen here billowing from a power plant in Shenyang, China—contributes to climate change, the author argues that catastrophic global warming does not exist.

A hectoring phrase like "unambiguous security threat" is supposed to dispel all doubts. Instead, it should create them, foreshadowing an administration that will treat the nation's security and economy frivolously.

Fiddling around with the economy for the sake of nothing more than advancing chic conjecture is the last thing an America in recession needs. Yet the Obama administration has already signaled that it will saddle slumping businesses with a global warming tax and onerous regulations, whenever the chance to sign a Kyoto-style treaty presents itself, perhaps in Copenhagen soon.

In all the talk these days about scams and bogus claims at the expense of shareholders and taxpayers, why doesn't the global warming activism of opportunistic CEOs and pols receive any scrutiny? It belongs to this age of fictions and dubious collusions between government and business.

The Democrats bemoan the alarmism that led America to war, yet practice it on global warming, with John Kerry recycling the Bush administration's risks-of-inaction cliché. By now we should know that in American politics nothing is as risky as action.

According to Hillary's testimony, climate change "threatens our very existence," before she put forward another modest assertion: "But well before that point, it could well incite wars of an old kind over basic resources—like food, water, and arable land."

It looks like Hillary is borrowing a page from her old friend, Timothy Wirth, the Clinton administration State Department official who once let the cat out of the bag by touting the ideological benefits of reckless alarmism: "What we've got to do in energy conservation is try to ride the global warming issue. Even if the theory of global warming is wrong, to have approached global warming as if it is real means energy conservation, so we will be doing the right thing anyway in terms of economic policy and environmental policy."

In order to scam the nation into statism, liberals know that they cannot afford to hedge their rhetoric or be too circumspect in their assertions. Al Gore's inconvenient half-baked opinion had to be called "An Inconvenient Truth," lest anyone doubt the necessity of accepting a "truth." Now Hillary and Kerry ratchet global warming theory's status up even more, to that of "unambiguous security threat."

At Davos a couple years back, Bill Clinton, yielding to no one in his capacity for concern, declared that global warming "is the only thing that I believe has the power to fundamentally end the march of civilization as we know it."

If a threat to the future of civilization exists, it will come not from the environment but from environmentalists. An extortionist agenda that

"Rescue from climate change," cartoon by Eric Allie, CagleCartoons.com, April 27, 2008. Copyright © 2008 Eric Allie, CagleCartoons.com and PoliticalCartoons.com.

What Are the Most Serious Threats to National Security?   49

will bankrupt industries (as Obama glibly warned the coal industry in an interview with the *San Francisco Chronicle* during the campaign) and creeping world government pose the gravest threats.

Hillary, Kerry, and Obama are acting like a committee of Greek Gods who will control the weather for the world. "President-elect Obama has said America must be a leader in developing and implementing a global and coordinated response to climate change," Hillary said in her testimony.

Stocking his administration with global warming activists, Obama senses that this issue could give full range to his ambitions. It is certainly an issue which lends itself to the apocalyptic rhetoric that surrounds him—that he, as the liberal columnist Mark Morford once put it, could "actually help usher in a new way of being on the planet."

While Hillary Clinton may not want to feed those ambitions, she does see global warming alarmism as a path to ideological ones. Christine Stewart, the former Canadian Minister of the Environment, would have understood Hillary's game in calling global warming an "unambiguous security threat."

"No matter if the science is phony, there are collateral environmental benefits," Stewart has said. "Climate change [provides] the greatest chance to bring about justice and equality in the world."

EVALUATING THE AUTHORS' ARGUMENTS:

In this viewpoint, Neumayr states that catastrophic climate change does not exist. Compare this view with the previous viewpoint by the CNA Corporation. What evidence does each present that catastrophic global warming actually does or does not exist? Is the evidence from scientific research or does it take some other form?

Viewpoint

7

Nuclear Proliferation Is a Threat to National Security

Graham Allison

"The likelihood of a single nuclear bomb exploding in a single city is greater today than at the height of the Cold War."

In the following viewpoint Graham Allison argues that nuclear proliferation—the spread of nuclear weapons—is a grave threat to America's security. He explains that several countries, especially North Korea and Iran, are probably developing nuclear weapons to use against their enemies. Both countries have a tenuous relationship with the United States, and if the relationship breaks down further, Allison worries that North Korean or Iranian leaders might choose to explode a nuclear bomb on American soil or sell the technology to terrorists. Allison also fears that terrorists like al Qaeda could steal nuclear materials and make their own bomb. A single bomb exploded in a metropolis like New York City could have devastating consequences, killing hundreds of thousands of people. Allison says the United States must keep Americans

Graham Allison, "The Will to Prevent: Global Challenges of Nuclear Proliferation," *Harvard International Review*, Fall 2006, pp. 50–56. Copyright © 2006 *The Harvard International Review*. Reproduced by permission.

safe by working with other nations to stop the development and spread of nuclear weapons.

Allison is the founding dean of Harvard's John F. Kennedy School of Government and director of the Belfer Center for Science and International Affairs. He also served as assistant secretary of defense in the first administration of President Bill Clinton.

AS YOU READ, CONSIDER THE FOLLOWING QUESTIONS:
1. Allison estimates that North Korea has enough plutonium for how many nuclear weapons?
2. By what percentage must uranium be enriched to create a nuclear bomb core, according to Allison?
3. What country does Allison say financed Pakistan's secret nuclear weapons program in the 1980s?

Imagine that on September 11, 2006, the fifth anniversary of the September 11 attacks, terrorists successfully executed a nuclear terrorist attack in New York City. On a normal working day, more than 500,000 people crowd the area within a half-mile radius of Times Square. The explosion of a Hiroshima-sized nuclear device [dropped on Hiroshima, Japan, in 1945] in midtown Manhattan would have killed all of them instantly. Hundreds of thousands of others would have died in the hours thereafter. The blast would have generated temperatures reaching 540,000 degrees Fahrenheit, instantly vaporizing the Theater District, the New York Times Building, and Grand Central Terminal. The ensuing firestorm would have stretched from Rockefeller Center to the Empire State Building, and buildings from the Metropolitan Museum near 80th street and the Flatiron Building near 20th street would have looked like the Murrah Federal Office Building following the Oklahoma City bombing [of 1995].

The Threat of Nuclear Proliferation
With the recent North Korean nuclear test bringing nuclear danger into sharp relief, many citizens are now asking: how real is the threat of terrorists exploding a nuclear bomb and devastating a great metropolis?

Nuclear Weapons Pose the Greatest Threat

A survey of more than one hundred top foreign policy experts said nuclear weapons and materials pose the greatest threat to national security.

Question: In your view, what is the single greatest threat to U.S. national security?	
Nuclear materials/weapons	20
Islamicism/al Qaeda/Jihadists	18
Terrorism	10
Economic decline	10
Weapons of mass destruction (WMDs)	7
U.S. leaders/Intelligence failures/Unilateralism/Overreaction	7
Overextended U.S./Inability to meet multiple challenges/Loss of purpose/Complacency	6
China	5
Climate change	3
Pakistan	3
Iran	2
Oil dependency	2
Ignorance/Fear of terrorism	1
Collapse of dollar	1
Russia	1
Non-state groups/actors	1
N/A/no response	3

Taken from: *Foreign Policy*, "The Terrorism Index," May 2008.

Former US Senator Sam Nunn believes the likelihood of a single nuclear bomb exploding in a single city is greater today than at the height of the Cold War. I believe the chances of a nuclear terrorist attack in the next decade are greater than 50 percent, given current trends. Former Secretary of Defense William Perry believes I underestimate the risk of an attack. Warren Buffet, the world's most successful investor, believes a nuclear terrorist attack "will happen. It's inevitable. I don't see any way that it won't happen." Companies that sell catastrophic terrorism insurance exclude nuclear attacks from their policies. Otherwise these insurance companies would be "vulnerable to extinction," in Buffett's words.

In April [2006], Bill Emmott stepped down from the helm of *The Economist* after 13 years as its leader. As is the tradition at *The Economist*, his final act was a substantial review of developments in the world during his tenure. In his essay, Emmott noted the unbelievable pace and extent of globalization that has occurred over the last 13 years. As he looked to the future, his forecast was faster and deeper globalization. But in conclusion, he asked: what could upset that forecast and even reverse the trend? His answer: a single nuclear bomb exploding in any capital in the world.

The face of nuclear danger today [2006] is a nuclear September 11. As Nobel Prize winner and head of the IAEA [International Atomic Energy Agency] Mohamed ElBaradei has warned, "The threat of nuclear terrorism is real and current." UN [United Nations] Secretary-General Kofi Annan noted, "Nuclear terrorism is still often treated as science fiction. I wish it were. But unfortunately we live in a world of excess hazardous materials and abundant technological know-how, in which some terrorists clearly state their intention to inflict catastrophic casualties. . . . Were a nuclear terrorist attack to occur, it would cause not only widespread death and destruction, but would stagger the world economy and thrust tens of millions of people into dire poverty." . . .

In preparing for the 60th anniversary of the United Nations, Secretary-General Kofi Annan established a panel of leading thinkers to assess global threats to the world's more than six billion people. The Commission gave primacy of place to renewed nuclear danger, driven by the proliferation of nuclear weapons and the possibility of nuclear terrorist attacks, warning starkly that the nonproliferation regime has eroded to the point of "irreversibility" that could trigger a "cascade of proliferation." How might such a catastrophic cascade occur? Simply by continuing the trends of the past decade.

North Korea Could Make Nuclear Weapons

North Korea's nuclear test on October 9 [2006] announced the arrival of a "new nuclear age," in the words of Japanese Prime Minister Shinzo Abe. Like a bolt of lightning that illuminates the landscape, this blast exposes deep fissures in the regime that has held back the nuclear tide for more than four decades. In essence, [North Korean leader] Kim Jong-Il has forced entry into the nuclear club, and his successful defiance will fuel further challenges to the international system and the global nuclear order.

North Korea has successfully defied not just its NPT [Nuclear Nonproliferation Treaty] commitment and the IAEA, but the United States, China, and the world. US intelligence analysts now estimate that North Korea has enough plutonium for eight to ten weapons. This includes two weapons' worth that went missing in 1999; six bombs' worth that had been frozen in warehouses under the 1994

North Korean soldiers condemn the UN's rebuke of the country's latest nuclear test. The author says North Korea could give its nuclear bomb technology to terrorists.

Agreed Framework[1] and constantly inspected by the IAEA until 2003 when North Korea withdrew from the Nuclear Nonproliferation Treaty; and two bombs' worth of material in spent fuel unloaded in February 2006. The Yongbyon reactor, on standby for most of the 90's, is now churning out enough plutonium for two more bombs a year. If, despite unambiguous warnings to North Korea, the United States and the world cannot roll back Pyongyang's nuclear advances, the United States' ability to deter the North from using a weapon will be in doubt.

East Asia and Iran May Acquire Nuclear Weapons

The governments of Japan, South Korea, and Taiwan have so far reiterated their societies' long-standing commitment to reject nuclear weapons. Nonetheless, my best bet is that over the decade ahead, both Japan and South Korea will arm themselves with nuclear weapons—undermining the security and stability that has been the foundation of East Asia's extraordinary economic growth.

Meanwhile, Iran is testing the line in the Middle East. On its current trajectory, the Islamic Republic will become a nuclear weapons state before the end of the decade. According to the leadership in Tehran, Iran is exercising its "inalienable right" to build uranium enrichment plants and make fuel for its peaceful civilian nuclear power generators. These same facilities, however, can continue enriching uranium to 90 percent U-235, which is the ideal core of a nuclear bomb. No one in the international community doubts that Iran's hidden objective in building enrichment facilities is to build nuclear bombs. If Iran crosses its nuclear finish line, a Middle Eastern cascade of new nuclear weapons states could trigger the first multi-party nuclear arms race, far more volatile than the Cold War competition between the United States and the Soviet Union.

A Nuclear Arms Race in the Middle East Is Dangerous

Given Egypt's historic role as the leader of the Arab Middle East, the prospects of it living unarmed alongside a nuclear Persia are very low. The IAEA's reports of clandestine nuclear experiments hint that Cairo

---

1. An agreement between the United States and North Korea that halted construction of nuclear reactors suspected of being part of a weapons program.

may have considered this possibility. Were Saudi Arabia to buy a dozen nuclear warheads that could be mated to the Chinese medium-range ballistic missiles it purchased secretly in the 1980s, few in the US intelligence community would be surprised. Given Saudi Arabia's role as the major financier of Pakistan's clandestine nuclear program in the 1980s, it is not out of the question that Riyadh and Islamabad have made secret arrangements for this contingency.

Such a multi-party nuclear arms race in the Middle East would be like playing Russian roulette—dramatically increasing the likelihood of a regional nuclear war. Other nightmare scenarios for the region include an accidental or unauthorized nuclear launch from Iran, theft of nuclear warheads from an unstable regime in Tehran, and possible Israeli preemption against Iran's nuclear facilities, which Israeli Prime Minister Ehud Olmert has implied, threatening, "Under no circumstances, and at no point, can Israel allow anyone with these kinds of malicious designs against us to have control of weapons of destruction that can threaten our existence."

Fast Fact

In 2009 the Federation of American Scientists reported that the world's combined stockpile of nuclear warheads totaled more than 23,300. Of these, more than 8,190 warheads are considered operational.

Toward Nuclear Responsibility

The largely unrecognized good news is that nuclear terrorism is preventable by a feasible, affordable checklist of actions. The strategic narrows in this challenge is to prevent terrorists from acquiring nuclear weapons or the materials from which weapons could be made. As a fact of physics: no highly enriched uranium or plutonium, no nuclear bomb, no nuclear terrorism. It is that simple. A strategy for pursuing that agenda can be organized under a "Doctrine of Three No's": No Loose Nukes, No New Nascent Nukes and No New Nuclear Weapons States. . . .

The 20th century's leading business thinker, Peter Drucker, frequently warned, "Plans are only good intentions unless they immediately degenerate into hard work." The painful truth is that failure to prevent the spread of nuclear weapons and the use of such weapons by terrorists would result from a failure of will, not of means. Having enjoyed six decades without the use of nuclear weapons as a result of the strenuous, steady actions of courageous leaders, this generation of leaders must ask what excuse it will give its successors if it bequeaths to them a world of nuclear anarchy.

EVALUATING THE AUTHOR'S ARGUMENTS:

Allison describes what would happen if terrorists dropped a nuclear bomb on New York City. His dramatic description is intended to show the reader how dangerous nuclear weapons really are. In your opinion, is this an effective technique? Does his example help convince you that nuclear weapons pose a serious threat to America's safety, or do you feel his description is a scare tactic? Explain your point of view using evidence from the text.

The Threat of Nuclear Proliferation Has Been Exaggerated

John Mueller

"Concern [over nuclear proliferation] is understandable, but it is overwrought and has had undesirable consequences."

In the following viewpoint John Mueller argues that the threat of nuclear proliferation has been exaggerated. For one thing, very few nations actually have nuclear weapons, and the number of these willing to use such weapons is even smaller. He explains that many nations have reversed or abandoned their nuclear weapons programs in the interest of pursuing peaceful relations with their neighbors. Others have complied with international treaties that seek to reduce the planet's nuclear weapons arsenal. Since fewer and fewer countries are making such weapons, Mueller argues that the threat from such weapons is diminishing. Furthermore, Mueller says it is highly unlikely that rogue nations such as Iran or North Korea would share nuclear weapons with terrorists. Reports that terrorist groups like al Qaeda (Al-Qaeda) have obtained nuclear weapons have been found to be mere rumors, and even if terrorists could obtain nuclear material, they lack the technical skills and know-how to make a bomb. Mueller concludes that there is little evidence that nuclear proliferation is a serious risk to U.S. national security, and promoting hysteria about it does more harm than good.

Mueller is a professor of political science at Ohio State University. He is also the author of *The Remnants of War* and *Overblown*, which examine the exaggerations of the international threat of terrorism.

AS YOU READ, CONSIDER THE FOLLOWING QUESTIONS:
1. How many nuclear warheads does Mueller say al Qaeda purchased from Chechen mobsters over a decade ago? Where does the author say these warheads are today?
2. According to Mueller, how many years did it take Pakistan to acquire enough fissile material to make an atomic bomb?
3. What five countries does Mueller say have reversed their nuclear weapons programs?

L et me be clear at the outset (since it will likely be forgotten by readers who manage to get past this paragraph) that I consider dissuading more countries from obtaining nuclear weapons to be quite a good idea and preventing terrorists from getting them to be an even better one. Indeed, I am even persuaded from time to time that the world might well be better off if the countries who now have them gave them up. Perhaps we could start with the French, who cling to an arsenal presumably under the imaginative notion that the weapons might one day prove useful should Nice be savagely bombarded from the sea or should a truly unacceptable number of Africans in former French colonies take up English.

It Is Not Productive to Obsess Over Nuclear Weapons
My concern, however, is that the obsessive quest to control nuclear proliferation—particularly since the end of the Cold War—has been substantially counterproductive and has often inflicted dire costs. Specifically, the effort to prevent proliferation has enhanced the appeal

of—or desperate desire for—nuclear weapons for some regimes, even as it has resulted in far more deaths than have been caused by all nuclear—or even all Weapons of Mass Destruction [WMDs]—detonations in all of history.

Presidents, White House hopefuls, congressmen, those in the threat-assessment business and the American public are convinced the biggest danger to the United States, and perhaps even the entire world order, comes from the two-pronged threat of nuclear proliferation and nuclear terrorism. This concern is understandable, but it is overwrought and has had undesirable consequences. . . .

Most States Would Not Risk Giving Terrorists a Nuclear Bomb

Here is [a] favorite fantasy of the alarmists: A newly nuclear country will pass a bomb or two to friendly terrorists for delivery abroad. Yet as William Langewiesche stresses in *Atomic Bazaar: The Rise of the Nuclear Poor*, this is highly improbable. There would be too much risk, even for a country led by extremists. If the ultimate source of the weapon were discovered—whether before or after detonation—international retribution could be unfathomably fierce. Potential detection as a nuclear-terrorist abettor carries too high a price. Moreover, no state is likely to trust Al-Qaeda—most are already on its extensive enemies list.

Since they are unlikely to be aided by an established state, terrorists would need to buy or steal the crucial fissile material [capable of undergoing nuclear fission] and then manufacture the device themselves. On this front, there is much rumor but little substance. Even though [Al-Qaeda leader Osama] Bin Laden sometimes appears to talk a good game, the degree to which Al-Qaeda has pursued a nuclear-weapons program may have been exaggerated by the arch-terrorist himself, as well as by the same slam-dunkers who packaged [former Iraqi dictator] Saddam's WMD-development scare.

Al-Qaeda's Nuclear Capabilities Are Exaggerated

The 9/11 Commission, media and various threat-mongers have trotted out evidence ranging from the ludicrous to the merely dubious when it comes to Al-Qaeda's nuclear intentions. One particularly well-worn tale—based on the testimony of an embezzling Al-Qaeda operative who later defected—describes Bin Laden's efforts to obtain some uranium while in Sudan in 1993. For his prize-winning book, *The Looming Tower*, Lawrence Wright interviewed two relevant people—including the man who supposedly made the purchase—and both say the episode never happened.

Then there are the two sympathetic Pakistani nuclear scientists who met with top Al-Qaeda leaders in Afghanistan in August 2001. Pakistani intelligence officers say the scientists found Bin Laden to be "intensely interested" in chemical, biological and nuclear weapons, but insist that the talks were wide-ranging and "academic," likely rendering little critical help on bomb design.

In what would seem to be other frightening news, a hand-written 25-page document entitled "Superbomb" was found in the home of

As evidence that it is hard to obtain nuclear weapons, the author discusses an alleged meeting between Pakistani nuclear scientist Sultan Bashir-ud-Din Mehmood (pictured) and al Qaeda, which led nowhere.

an Al-Qaeda leader in Afghanistan. But according to physicist David Albright, some sections are sophisticated while others are "remarkably inaccurate and naive." Many critical steps for making a nuclear weapon are missing; the bomb design figures, "not credible." In short, the entire program seems "relatively primitive."

When in full-on fantasyland, we even worry about decade-old reports of Al-Qaeda's purchase of twenty nuclear warheads from Chechen mobsters for $30 million and two tons of opium. And then there's the supposed acquisition of nuclear suitcase bombs in Russia, asserted by Al-Qaeda's second in command, Ayman al-Zawahiri, on the eve of Al-Qaeda's collapse in Afghanistan. Given the circumstances, this seems a desperate bluff, and it has been much disputed by Moscow officials and experts on the Russian program. Even if they still exist, these Soviet-era bombs have a short shelf life and today are nothing more than "radioactive scrap metal."

Terrorists Do Not Have Nuclear Material

Of course, absence of evidence, we need hardly be reminded, is not evidence of absence. Thus, [Harvard political scientist Graham] Allison reports that, when no abandoned nuclear-weapons material was found in Afghanistan, some intelligence analysts responded: "We haven't found most of Al-Qaeda's leadership either, and we know that they exist." Since we know Mount Rushmore exists, maybe the tooth fairy does as well.

Even if there is some desire for the bomb, fulfilling that desire is another matter. Though Allison assures us that it would be "easy" for terrorists to assemble a crude bomb if they could get enough fissile material, we see how difficult it is for states to acquire these capabilities (it took Pakistan 27 years)—let alone the Lone Ranger. Al-Qaeda would need people with great technical skills, a bevy of corrupted but utterly reliable co-conspirators and an implausible amount of luck to go undetected for months, if not years while developing and delivering their capabilities.

Perhaps aware of these monumental difficulties, terrorists around the world seem in effect to be heeding the advice found in a memo on an Al-Qaeda laptop seized in Pakistan in 2004: "Make use of that which is available . . . rather than waste valuable time becoming despondent over that which is not within your reach." That is, "Keep it simple, stupid."

Nuclear Proliferation Has Been Slow

Considering all the false scares and attendant unnecessary civilian casualties they've engendered, it may be time to think a bit about the strategic consequences of treating nuclear proliferation as the "supreme priority" of foreign policy.

As Langewiesche points out, the nuclear genie is out of the bottle, and just about any state can eventually obtain nuclear weapons if it really wants to make the effort—although in many cases that might involve, as a former president of Pakistan once colorfully put it, "eating grass" to pay for it.

Despite the predictions of generations of alarmists, nuclear proliferation has proceeded at a remarkably slow pace. In 1958 the National Planning Association predicted "a rapid rise in the number of atomic powers . . . by the mid-1960s", and a couple of years later, [President] John Kennedy observed that there might be "ten, fifteen, twenty" countries with a nuclear capacity by 1964. But over the decades a huge number of countries capable of developing nuclear weapons has not done so—Canada, Sweden and Italy, for example—and several others—Brazil, Argentina, South Africa, South Korea and Taiwan—have backed away from or reversed nuclear-weapons programs.

> **FAST FACT**
>
> According to the Commission on the Prevention of Weapons of Mass Destruction Proliferation and Terrorism, 95 percent of all nuclear material that could be used to make nuclear weapons is found in Russia and the United States.

There is, then, no imperative for countries to obtain nuclear weapons once they have achieved the appropriate technical and economic capacity to do so. Insofar as states that considered acquiring the weapons, they came to appreciate several defects: The weapons are dangerous, distasteful, costly and likely to rile the neighbors. If one values economic growth and prosperity above all, the sensible thing is to avoid the weapons unless they seem vital for security. . . .

Few Countries Have Nuclear Weapons

Just nine nations possess nuclear weapons. Several countries have been persuaded to abandon their weapons programs or have been deterred from starting them, and just one nation—North Korea—has become a nuclear power in this century. Some argue that, as a result, the threat of nuclear war is lower than ever.

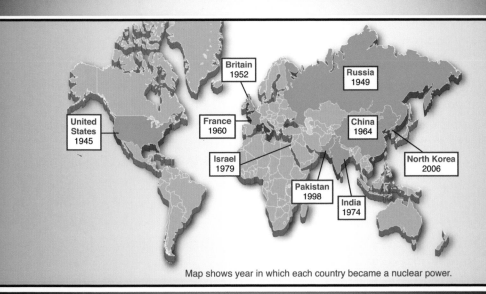

Britain
1952

Russia
1949

United
States
1945

France
1960

China
1964

North Korea
2006

Israel
1979

Pakistan
1998

India
1974

Map shows year in which each country became a nuclear power.

Taken from: Federation of American Scientists, 2009.

Nuclear Weapons Are Used to Deter

It is certainly preferable that none of these regimes (and quite a few others) ever obtain nuclear weapons. But if they do so they are by far most likely to put them to use the same way other nuclear countries have: to deter.

Nonetheless, even threatened states may not develop nuclear weapons. In the wake of the Iraq disaster, an invasion by the ever-threatening Americans can probably now be credibly deterred simply by maintaining a trained and well-armed cadre of a few thousand troops dedicated to, and capable of, inflicting endless irregular warfare on the hapless and increasingly desperate and ridiculous invaders. The Iranians do not yet seem to have grasped this new reality, but perhaps others on the [George W.] Bush Administration's implicit hit list will.

Alarmists about proliferation (which seems to include almost the totality of the foreign-policy establishment) may occasionally grant that countries principally obtain a nuclear arsenal to counter real or perceived threats. But many go on to argue that newly nuclear countries will then use nuclear weapons to dominate the area. This argument was repeatedly used with dramatic urgency for the dangers to world peace and order supposedly posed by Saddam Hussein, and it is now being dusted off and applied to Iran.

Exactly how this domination business is to be carried out is never made very clear. The United States possesses a tidy array of thousands of nuclear weapons and can't even dominate downtown Baghdad—or even keep the lights on there. But the notion apparently is that should an atomic Iraq (in earlier fantasies) or Iran (in present ones) rattle the occasional rocket, all other countries in the area, suitably intimidated, would supinely bow to its demands. Far more likely is that they will make common cause with each other against the threatening neighbor, perhaps enlisting the convenient aid eagerly proffered by other countries, probably including the United States and conceivably even Israel.

Nuclear Proliferation Is Not a Serious Threat

Proliferation of the bomb, particularly to terrorists, may indeed be the single most serious threat to the national security of the United States. Assessed in appropriate context, that could actually be seen as a rather cheering conclusion.

EVALUATING THE AUTHORS' ARGUMENTS:

John Mueller argues that making a nuclear weapon requires hard-to-get materials, extensive knowledge, and the ability to go undetected in the process. As such, he calls Graham Allison, the author of the preceding viewpoint, an "alarmist" for saying that terrorists could easily make a nuclear bomb. Do you think it is a fair characterization? Why or why not?

Chapter 2

How Can the United States Best Achieve National Security?

In San Jose, California, airline passengers are forced to surrender water bottles, toothpaste, and other sundries due to increased security at airports. Some say that security requirements have gone too far.

Wiretapping and Other Security Measures Keep America Safe

Stuart Taylor Jr.

"Our way of life may well depend on catching nuclear or biological terrorists before they can strike. And the only way to catch them is through aggressive use of wiretaps."

In the following viewpoint Stuart Taylor Jr. argues that wiretapping and other security measures keep America safe from terrorists. Taylor says that tools such as wiretapping, data mining, searches and seizures, detention, interrogation, and other forms of surveillance expose where terrorists are hiding and whether they are planning an attack on innocent Americans. Without these security tools, Taylor says, it is nearly impossible to locate terrorists or figure out what they are planning. Taylor promises that these tools do not violate the privacy or rights of law-abiding Americans and are well within the bounds of the Constitution. Taylor concludes that the U.S. government has an obligation to protect Americans using any means possible and should take advantage of wiretapping and other security measures to do so.

Taylor is a regular columnist for the *National Journal*, a contributing editor at *Newsweek*, and a nonresident senior fellow in governance studies at the Brookings Institution.

AS YOU READ, CONSIDER THE FOLLOWING QUESTIONS:
1. According to Taylor, by what year might a weapon of mass destruction be used in a terrorist attack somewhere in the world?
2. How many innocent people does Taylor say have been seriously harmed by the government's abuse of wiretapping, surveillance, or data mining?
3. What does the term "suicide pact" mean in the context of the viewpoint?

President-elect Obama's announcement of his (mostly) stellar national security team coincides with the release this week of a bipartisan commission report with this chilling assessment of the most important challenge that team faces: "Without greater urgency and decisive action by the world community, it is more likely than not that a weapon of mass destruction will be used in a terrorist attack somewhere in the world by the end of 2013."

Perhaps the commission, former Defense Secretary William Perry, and other experts who have issued similarly dramatic warnings are crying wolf. Perhaps the likelihood of any terrorist group getting a nuclear bomb is "vanishingly small," as Ohio State political science professor John Mueller has forcefully argued. Or perhaps it's closer to 30 percent over the next 10 years, as Matthew Bunn of Harvard's Kennedy School estimated last month in "Securing the Bomb 2008."

Whatever the odds, if terrorists ever smuggle a crude, Hiroshima-sized nuke into, say, Manhattan, the immediate death toll could exceed 500,000. And the ensuing panic could threaten our constitutional system, spur evacuations of major cities, kill international trade, bring the worst economic depression in history, and perhaps usher in a new dark age worldwide.

This prospect puts into perspective the efforts of many human-rights activists, Obama supporters, and journalists to weaken essentially *all* of the government's most important tools for disabling terrorists before they can strike.

Wiretaps? These folks would make it far easier for terrorists to escape detection, by greatly narrowing the government's electronic surveillance powers. Data mining through reams of commercial records in search of terrorist trails? Ditto. Detention of suspected "enemy combatants" who are very dangerous but cannot be criminally convicted? Release them! Interrogation of terrorist leaders? Just say no, even to mild forms of coercion such as angry yelling and threats. The USA PATRIOT Act? Repeal key provisions. FBI guidelines? Ban the feds from focusing more investigative resources on young Arab men from overseas than on African-American grandmothers.

Civil libertarians are rightly outraged by the brutality of some Bush administration interrogation methods; by Bush's denial of fair hearings to hundreds of suspects at Guantanamo and elsewhere who claim that they are not terrorists; and by his years of secretly and perhaps illegally defying—rather than asking Congress to amend—the badly outdated Foreign Intelligence Surveillance Act.

But the civil libertarians' outrage does not stop there. Indeed, the prospect of anyone in the U.S. being inappropriately wiretapped, surveilled, or data-mined seems to stir the viscera of many Bush critics more than the prospect of thousands of people being murdered by terrorists. This despite the paucity of evidence that any innocent person anywhere has been seriously harmed in recent decades by governmental abuse of wiretapping, surveillance, or data mining.

On these and similar issues, Obama will have a choice: He can give the Left what it wants and weaken our defenses. Or he can follow the advice of his more prudent advisers, recognize that Congress, the courts, and officials including Attorney General Michael Mukasey have already moved to end the worst Bush administration abuses—and kick the hard Left gently in the teeth. I'm betting that Obama is smart and tough enough to do the latter.

This is not to suggest that the president-elect will or should condone torture, bypass Congress, disregard international law and opinion, or adopt other Bush excesses that Obama and Attorney General–designate Eric Holder have assailed. But Obama does need to claim and use far more muscular powers to avert catastrophic loss of life and protect our security than most human-rights activists (and most Europeans) would allow.

The recommendations in the 112-page report quoted above—issued by the congressionally established Commission on the Prevention of Weapons of Mass Destruction Proliferation and Terrorism—focus mainly on the need for greater efforts to prevent WMD from falling into terrorist hands. Such efforts are critical, but at best cannot eliminate the threat. So our way of life may well depend on catching nuclear or biological terrorists before they can strike.

And the only way to catch them is through aggressive use of wiretaps, data mining, searches, seizures, other forms of surveillance, detention, interrogation, subpoenas, informants, and, sometimes, group-based profiling. Many of these powers and techniques are still tightly restricted by the web of legal restraints and media-driven cultural norms that were developed in sunnier times to protect civil liberties—and would be even more tightly restricted if civil libertarians had their way.

I sketch below how Obama should strike the liberty-security balance in three areas; in future columns I will focus on these and related issues in more detail.

Wiretapping and data mining: Civil libertarians and most congressional Democrats have complained that the government has too much power to intercept phone calls and e-mails in search of terrorists, under the amendments to the Foreign Intelligence Surveillance Act that were adopted this summer. In fact, the government still has too little power to intercept communications and at the same time too few safeguards against misuse of the information.

FISA, which has always required judicial permission based on "probable cause" to target calls and e-mails between parties inside the U.S. but not calls from or to targets outside the U.S., is badly outdated: It is often impossible to tell where the parties to a cellphone call or an e-mail are. In addition, "the surveillance it authorizes is unusable to discover who is a terrorist, as distinct from eavesdropping on known terrorists—yet the former is the more urgent task," as Judge Richard Posner has written.

Obama, a harsh critic of Bush's secret, unilateral defiance of FISA's rules from 2001 through 2005, wisely broke with most liberals by voting in July to relax those rules. He should propose a complete overhaul and simplification of the almost incomprehensibly complicated law. It should be easier to use sophisticated computer data-mining programs to fish through millions of calls and e-mails for signs of possible terrorist activity. At the same time, privacy protections should be improved by tightening the rules to detect (through use of audit trails) and prevent unnecessary dissemination or retention of the intercepted information and to punish severely any misuse of it. An additional privacy protection, suggested by Posner, would be to forbid use of this information for any purpose (including, say, tax fraud prosecutions) other than to protect national security.

Detainees: Obama should keep his promise to close the Guantanamo prison camp, within a year if possible, and should release as soon as possible and urge Congress to compensate all detainees who are found to be both nondangerous and nonprosecutable. Although Guantanamo is now about as humane as a prison housing some extremely dangerous terrorists could be, its ugly history has made it a worldwide symbol of detention without due process and brutal treatment of detainees, including many mistakenly captured innocents. Obama should also end Bush's misbegotten system of "military commissions" to put detainees on trial for suspected war crimes, and instead should try as many as possible in ordinary military or civilian courts.

But Obama should spurn the clamor from the Left to simply release any and all of the more than 240 remaining detainees who cannot be criminally convicted. Instead, he should establish a blue-ribbon, bipartisan commission to study all the available evidence on each detainee. Many may turn out to be both extremely dangerous and impossible to convict of crimes, as the military claims, because of strict rules of evidence and other obstacles. Obama should continue to detain that group, probably in U.S. lockups, while working with Congress to establish a new process to give these men every possible opportunity to challenge the factual and legal bases for their continued detention.

Interrogation: Obama should promptly issue an executive order reinforcing the criminal ban on torturing detainees and imposing a

The author urges President Barack Obama to close the detention center at Guantánamo Bay, Cuba, and in May 2009 the president announced his intention to do so.

general rule against harsh methods. He should also direct the Justice Department to revoke or revise any as-yet-unrevoked legal opinions taking an unduly narrow view of the anti-torture law. But for reasons discussed in my May 3 column, he should preserve the option of using coercive methods short of torture in especially urgent cases, if the attorney general personally approves. And he should ask himself: What would I want done if the CIA captures another terrorist mastermind such as Khalid Shaikh Mohammed, who is determined not to talk but whose secrets—if extracted—might well save many lives?

If Obama strikes judicious balances between security and liberty, the ACLU and its allies may hysterically accuse him (as they would certainly accuse any Republican president) of trashing the Constitution. But the vast majority of voters understand that the Constitution is not a suicide pact.

Meanwhile, like the prospect of a hanging, the prospect of a terrorist nuclear bomb obliterating downtown Washington—including the Obama family—or Manhattan will concentrate the president-elect's mind wonderfully.

EVALUATING THE AUTHORS' ARGUMENTS:

Taylor argues that law-abiding Americans are not negatively affected by wiretapping and other security measures. How do you think the author of the following viewpoint, Russ Feingold, might respond to this argument? Explain your answer using evidence from the texts.

Illegally Wiretapping Americans Does Not Keep the Nation Safe

Russ Feingold

"The President openly acknowledged that he has ordered the government to spy on Americans, on American soil, without the warrants required by law."

In the following viewpoint Russ Feingold argues that wiretapping and other security measures do not keep America safe. Feingold explains that the government has violated the Constitution and used counterterrorism tools to spy on innocent Americans. In many cases, the government has failed to get appropriate warrants needed to conduct surveillance on intelligence targets. Feingold argues that citizens cannot feel safe if their own government is violating their basic rights. He also wonders how American citizens can be kept safe from terrorists when they are not even safe from their own government. The author concludes that America cannot be a beacon of freedom to the rest of the world if it violates the freedoms of its own citizens at home.

Feingold is a U.S. Democratic senator from Wisconsin. He has served in the Senate since 1993.

Russ Feingold, "On the President's Warrantless Wiretapping Program," feingold.senate.gov, February 7, 2006. Reproduced by permission.

AS YOU READ, CONSIDER THE FOLLOWING QUESTIONS:

1. What amendment to the U.S. Constitution states that all Americans have the right to be free from unjustified government intrusions?
2. What American founder said, "Give me liberty or give me death"?
3. In what year was the Foreign Intelligence Surveillance Act passed?

L ast week [February 2006] the President of the United States [George W. Bush] gave his State of the Union address, where he spoke of America's leadership in the world, and called on all of us to "lead this world toward freedom." Again and again, he invoked the principle of freedom, and how it can transform nations, and empower people around the world.

But, almost in the same breath, the President openly acknowledged that he has ordered the government to spy on Americans, on American soil, without the warrants required by law.

The President issued a call to spread freedom throughout the world, and then he admitted that he has deprived Americans of one of their most basic freedoms under the Fourth Amendment—to be free from unjustified government intrusion. . . .

America's Wiretapping Program Is Illegal

The President suggests that anyone who criticizes his illegal wiretapping program doesn't understand the threat we face. But we do. Every single one of us is committed to stopping the terrorists who threaten us and our families.

Defeating the terrorists should be our top national priority, and we all agree that we need to wiretap them to do it. In fact, it would be irresponsible not to wiretap terrorists. But we have yet to see any reason why we have to trample the laws of the United States to do it. The President's decision that he can break the law says far more about his attitude toward the rule of law than it does about the laws themselves.

This goes way beyond party, and way beyond politics. What the President has done here is to break faith with the American people.

In the State of the Union, he also said that "we must always be clear in our principles" to get support from friends and allies that we need to fight terrorism. So let's be clear about a basic American principle: When someone breaks the law, when someone misleads the public in an attempt to justify his actions, he needs to be held accountable. The

"Orwell Man Bush Defends Wiretapping," cartoon by Andy Singer, PoliticalCartoons.com, January 16, 2006. © Copyright 2006 Andy Singer, PoliticalCartoons.com.

President of the United States has broken the law. The President of the United States is trying to mislead the American people. And he needs to be held accountable. . . .

Judges Should Review Wiretaps

In December [2005], we found out that the President has authorized wiretaps of Americans without the court orders required by law. He says he is only wiretapping people with links to terrorists, but how do we know? We don't. The President is unwilling to let a neutral judge make sure that is the case. He will not submit this program to an independent branch of government to make sure he's not violating the rights of law-abiding Americans.

So I don't want to hear again that this Administration has shown it can be trusted. It hasn't. And that is exactly why the law requires a judge to review these wiretaps. . . .

Americans' Basic Rights Have Been Violated

To find out that the President of the United States has violated the basic rights of the American people is chilling. And then to see him publicly embrace his actions—and to see so many Members of Congress cheer him on—is appalling.

The President has broken the law, and he has made it clear that he will continue to do so. But the President is not a king. And the Congress is not a king's court. Our job is not to stand up and cheer when the President breaks the law. Our job is to stand up and demand accountability, to stand up and check the power of an out-of-control executive branch.

That is one of the reasons that the framers put us here—to ensure balance between the branches of government, not to act as a professional cheering section.

It Is Not Necessary to Break the Law to Defend America

We need answers. Because no one, not the President, not the Attorney General, and not any of their defenders in this body [Congress], has been able to explain why it is necessary to break the law to defend against terrorism. And I think that's because they can't explain it.

Instead, this administration reacts to anyone who questions this illegal program by saying that those of us who demand the truth and stand up for our rights and freedoms have a pre-9/11 view of the world.

In fact, the President has a pre-1776 view of the world.

Our Founders lived in dangerous times, and they risked everything for freedom. Patrick Henry said, "Give me liberty or give me death." The President's pre-1776 mentality is hurting America. It is fracturing the foundation on which our country has stood for 230 years. The President can't just bypass two branches of government, and obey only those laws he wants to obey. Deciding unilaterally which of our freedoms still apply in the fight against terrorism is unacceptable and needs to be stopped immediately. . . .

FISA Issues Legal Wiretapping Warrants

The Foreign Intelligence Surveillance Act [FISA] was passed in 1978 to create a secret court, made up of judges who develop national security expertise, to issue warrants for surveillance of terrorists and spies. These are the judges from whom the Bush Administration has obtained thousands of warrants since 9/11. The Administration has almost never had a warrant request rejected by those judges. They have used the FISA Court thousands of times, but at the same time they assert that FISA is an "old law" or "out of date" and they can't comply with it. Clearly they can and do comply with it—except when they don't. Then they just arbitrarily decide to go around these judges, and around the law.

The Administration has said that it ignored FISA because it takes too long to get a warrant under that law. But we know that in an emergency, where the Attorney General believes that surveillance must begin before a court order can be obtained, FISA permits the wiretap to be executed immediately as long as the government goes to the court within 72 hours. The Attorney General has complained that the emergency provision does not give him enough flexibility, he has complained that getting a FISA application together or getting the necessary approvals takes too long. But the problems he has cited are bureaucratic barriers that the executive branch put in place, and could easily remove if it wanted.

FISA also permits the Attorney General to authorize unlimited warrantless electronic surveillance in the United States during the 15 days following a declaration of war, to allow time to consider any amendments to FISA required by a wartime emergency. That is the time period that Congress specified. Yet the President thinks that he can do this indefinitely. . . .

The President Knowingly Violated the Law

The President knows that FISA makes it a crime to wiretap Americans in the United States without a warrant or a court order. Why else would he have assured the public, over and over again, that he was getting warrants before engaging in domestic surveillance?

Here's what the President said on April 20, 2004: "Now, by the way, any time you hear the United States government talking about wiretap, it requires—a wiretap requires a court order. Nothing has changed, by the way. When we're talking about chasing down terrorists, we're talking about getting a court order before we do so."

And again, on July 14, 2004: "The government can't move on wiretaps or roving wiretaps without getting a court order."

The President was understandably eager in these speeches to make it clear that under his administration, law enforcement was using the FISA Court to obtain warrants before wiretapping. That is understandable, since wiretapping Americans on American soil without a warrant is against the law.

And listen to what the President said on June 9, 2005: "Law enforcement officers need a federal judge's permission to wiretap a foreign terrorist's phone, a federal judge's permission to track his calls, or a federal judge's permission to search his property. Officers must meet strict standards to use any of these tools. And these standards are fully consistent with the Constitution of the U.S."

Wisconsin Democrat and U.S. senator Russ Feingold, the viewpoint's author, has been a strong opponent of wiretapping.

Now that the public knows about the domestic spying program, he has had to change course. He has looked around for arguments to cloak his actions. And all of them are completely threadbare. . . .

Illegal Wiretapping Damages America's Reputation

None of the President's arguments explains or excuses his conduct, or the NSA's [National Security Agency's] domestic spying program. Not one. It is hard to believe that the President has the audacity to claim that they do. It is a strategy that really hinges on the credibility of the office of the Presidency itself. If you just insist that you didn't break the law, you haven't broken the law. It reminds me of what Richard Nixon said after he had left office: "Well, when the president does it that means that it is not illegal." But that is not how our constitutional democracy works. Making those kinds of arguments is damaging the credibility of the Presidency. . . .

Freedom Must Be Protected

The President's actions are indefensible. Freedom is an enduring principle. It is not something to celebrate in one breath, and ignore the next. Freedom is at the heart of who we are as a nation, and as a people. We cannot be a beacon of freedom for the world unless we protect our own freedoms here at home.

The President was right about one thing. In his address, he said "We love our freedom, and we will fight to keep it."

Yes, Mr. President. We do love our freedom, and we will fight to keep it. We will fight to defeat the terrorists who threaten the safety and security of our families and loved ones. And we will fight to protect the rights of law-abiding Americans against intrusive government power.

> ## EVALUATING THE AUTHOR'S ARGUMENTS:
>
> Russ Feingold argues that illegal wiretapping hurts America's democracy and makes Americans more vulnerable to terrorism. Clarify what he means by this. Do you think he is right? Explain your answer thoroughly.

No-Fly Lists Keep America Safe

Kip Hawley

"We are waging a broad and unrelenting war against terror."

The following viewpoint contains author Kip Hawley's September 9, 2008, testimony before the U.S. Congressional Committee on Homeland Security, Subcommittee on Transportation Security and Infrastructure Protection. Hawley argues that no-fly lists keep America safe. These are lists that contain the names of known or suspected terrorists who are deemed too dangerous to fly on commercial airlines. Hawley argues that no-fly lists help improve airport security and reduce the possibility that terrorists will take an airplane hostage, as they did on September 11, 2001. Hawley explains how the lists work: All passengers are screened prior to boarding an aircraft to see if any of their names are on the list. If so, those persons are considered to be a threat to national security and are not allowed to board the plane. Hawley describes how Secure Flight, a new watchlist program, promises to keep terrorists off airplanes while at the same time protecting the rights of innocent Americans. He concludes that no-fly lists are important national security tools in America's fight against terrorism.

Kip Hawley, "Testimony Before the Committee on Homeland Security, Subcommittee on Transportation Security and Infrastructure Protection," TSA.gov, September 9, 2008. Reproduced by permission.

Hawley is the former administrator for the Transportation Security Administration, under the U.S. Department of Homeland Security.

AS YOU READ, CONSIDER THE FOLLOWING QUESTIONS:
1. What database does Hawley say is one of the most important tools in the U.S. government's fight against terrorism?
2. How many people does Hawley say are on no-fly lists? How many of them are Americans?
3. According to Hawley, in what six ways will the Secure Flight program improve aviation security?

Thank you for the opportunity to appear before you today [September 9, 2008] on behalf of the Transportation Security Administration (TSA) and the Department of Homeland Security (DHS) to discuss our continuing efforts to improve the aviation security environment through the development of the Secure Flight program and to effectively use intelligence to prevent terrorists from using the transportation system to gain entry to or harm the United States. . . .

Screening Database Identifies Terrorists

The National Commission on Terrorist Attacks Upon the United States (9/11 Commission) placed a strong emphasis on enhancing the use of watchlists as part of a layered aviation security system. The 9/11 Commission's final report recommends that the watchlist matching function should be performed by TSA and that air carriers should be required to supply the information needed to test and implement this new system.

TSA's aviation security strategy relies upon an interlocking system of multiple layers of security. Key to this system is the use of intelligence to both develop countermeasures against terrorist threats and to intervene directly when threats become apparent. One of the most important tools in the fight against terrorism is the U.S. Government's consolidated Terrorist Screening Database (TSDB).

Prior to 9/11, information about known or suspected terrorists was dispersed throughout the U.S. Government, and no single agency was charged with consolidating it and making it available for use in terrorist screening. Under Homeland Security Presidential Directive

(HSPD) 6, the TSC [Terrorist Screening Center] now provides "one-stop shopping" so that every government agency is using the same TSDB—whether it is TSA, a U.S. consular official issuing visas overseas, or a State or local law enforcement officer on the street. The consolidated system allows government agencies to run name checks against one comprehensive database with the most accurate, up-to-date information about known and suspected terrorists.

The consolidated system provides the critical nexus between the work of the intelligence and law enforcement communities and the rest of the counterterrorism community. Our partners in the law enforcement and intelligence communities work tirelessly and in some cases under great physical danger to identify individuals who pose a terror threat. It would be dangerous and negligent not to use this information to our advantage. TSA is constantly adapting to the ever-changing threat environment and improving our people, processes, and technology to detect and deter threats. As important as it is to detect threat objects, it is imperative that we use intelligence to aid in the identification and interception of the people who would do us harm.

Keeping Terrorists off Airplanes

TSA utilizes subsets of the TSDB—the No Fly and Selectee lists. A nominating agency can recommend that a known or suspected terrorist be placed on the No Fly or Selectee list if the individual meets specific criteria for inclusion on that list.

A Transportation Security Administration employee uses a consolidated system that allows her to run name checks using a comprehensive database.

Terror watchlists keep legitimate terror threats off airplanes every day, all over the world. There are significantly fewer than 50,000 individuals on the No Fly and Selectee lists and only a small percentage of those are in the United States. The lists are reserved for known or suspected terrorists who have reached a threshold where they should not be allowed to fly or should receive additional scrutiny before boarding an aircraft. Using the No Fly and Selectee watchlists, TSA can quickly evaluate passengers to determine if they have a known or suspected link to terrorism or pose a threat to national security and to prevent passengers with known or suspected links to terrorism from boarding aircraft.

The No Fly and Selectee lists are made available for passenger prescreening to air carriers flying into, out of, or within the U.S. for passenger prescreening. As part of their shared responsibility for aviation security, air carriers play a critical role in ensuring that individuals on the No Fly list do not board aircraft. Air carriers must conduct watchlist checks in advance of issuance of boarding passes, and they must notify the TSA of a match to the No Fly list. TSA then notifies the TSC and the FBI, which coordinate the operational response with law enforcement and other agencies and foreign partners as appropriate. Air carriers must also ensure that a match to the Selectee list is subject to secondary screening prior to boarding an aircraft. Aside from a Selectee match, an individual may be subject to secondary screening based on the Computer-Assisted Passenger Prescreening Systems (CAPPS), as a result of our behavior detection officers, or through other random and unpredictable screening processes we have employed at the checkpoint as part of our layered security system. . . .

> # FAST FACT
>
> As of 2006, there were forty-four thousand names on the U.S. government's list of suspected terrorists banned from air travel, according to the National Security News Service and *60 Minutes*. Before 9/11, the list contained only sixteen names.

"Secure Flight" Will Improve Aviation Security

TSA is moving forward aggressively to assume responsibility for watchlist matching for both international and domestic air passengers through Secure Flight. Secure Flight will close a critical aviation security gap and

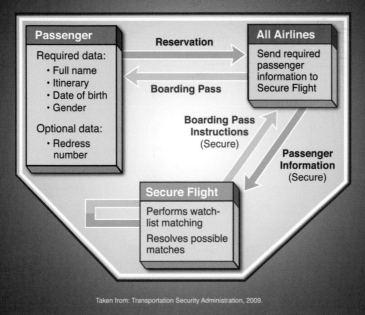

How No-Fly Lists Work

By cross-referencing passenger names with a list of people who are deemed too dangerous to fly, advocates say, programs like Secure Flight prevent terrorist attacks.

Passenger

Required data:
- Full name
- Itinerary
- Date of birth
- Gender

Optional data:
- Redress number

Reservation

Boarding Pass

All Airlines

Send required passenger information to Secure Flight

Boarding Pass Instructions (Secure)

Passenger Information (Secure)

Secure Flight

Performs watch-list matching

Resolves possible matches

Taken from: Transportation Security Administration, 2009.

reduce the vulnerabilities associated with watchlist matching performed by the airlines. Under Secure Flight, watchlist matching will be more effective, efficient, and consistent, offering improvements in both security and customer service for the traveling public. Secure Flight will add a vital layer of security to our nation's commercial air transportation system while maintaining the privacy of passenger information. TSA evaluated and realigned Secure Flight in 2006 to ensure that privacy and security serve as the very foundation for the system. The realignment established the basic infrastructure and fundamentals of a rigorous program including extensive program management elements. The effort ensured privacy practices are built into all areas of the program.

Secure Flight will improve aviation security by providing:
- Early knowledge of potential watchlist matches;
- Earlier law enforcement notification;
- Decreased chance of compromised watchlist data because of its limited distribution;

- Enhanced use of the Redress Process and Cleared List;
- Consistent watchlist matching process across all aircraft operators; and
- Privacy protections for individuals. . . .

The Secure Flight System Can Prevent Terrorist Attacks

Many aircraft operators expressed concerns about the proposed 60-day implementation period. TSA has modified the Secure Flight implementation approach to accommodate the needs for the industry to make changes to systems and processes. TSA has conducted a series of meetings and working sessions on topics including implementation strategy, testing, and outages, and these meetings will continue with the publication of the Final Rule. As we continue to ready Secure Flight for deployment and ensure a smooth transition through parallel testing of the system, we look forward to a continued partnership with the air carrier industry, with whom we share a common goal of keeping dangerous individuals off aircraft while facilitating legitimate passenger travel. . . .

TSA is making major strides toward implementation of Secure Flight, a step that will enhance transportation security and improve customer service while taking advantage of critical intelligence to prevent a terrorist act against the U.S.

EVALUATING THE AUTHOR'S ARGUMENTS:

Kip Hawley has worked as the administrator for the Transportation Security Administration, part of the U.S. Department of Homeland Security. Does knowing the author's credentials influence your opinion of his argument? Are you more likely to be convinced by his point of view because of the job he has held? Why or why not?

No-Fly Lists Do Not Keep America Safe

Faisal Kutty

"Common sense should make us wonder how someone can be too guilty to fly and yet be too innocent to be charged."

In the following viewpoint Faisal Kutty argues that no-fly lists do not keep America safe from terrorists. He acknowledges that no-fly lists were designed to protect Americans from terrorists by keeping them off airplanes and away from airports. However, Kutty asserts, no-fly lists just stop innocent citizens from flying and, as a result, infringe on their basic rights. He claims innocent people end up on these lists because their names are similar to those of terrorists. In addition, people with ethnic or religious-sounding names end up on lists, even when no evidence connects them to terrorists. Kutty argues that these lists have yet to capture a real terrorist; in fact, most terrorists are not even found on these lists, according to Kutty. The author concludes that no-fly lists do nothing to improve national security, and the government could better protect the United States by focusing its efforts on capturing real terrorists.

Kutty is a Toronto lawyer and adjunct professor at Osgoode Hall Law School of York University. He is also a visiting assistant professor at Valparaiso University School of Law.

"Nothing personal sir, but your packages are not allowed on passenger airlines," said a United Parcel Service [UPS] customer service agent, sitting in an American call centre. She was explaining to me that my package could not be delivered on an "early A.M." basis from Toronto [Canada] to Peterborough [New Hampshire].

I was interrogating the agent about why this was so, since I had been using UPS without any problems since starting my [law] practice in 1996. Initially reluctant, the agent eventually confessed that when my account number was entered into their system, the "Flight Guardian" software flashed a red signal.

"Sir," she said, "after 9/11 we can only pick up packages if the green light is given."

The next day I called the UPS head office and inquired about the situation. The supervisor apologized and informed me that I could use the expedited service within Canada, but that I did not have the requisite clearance to use this service to the U.S.

Troubling Development in the "War on Terror"

We will never know how many Canadians have been so specially designated on more than a dozen lists maintained by the United States. The proliferation of these watch lists around the globe has been a troubling development in the "war on terror."

Now the Canadian government may complicate the situation even more by introducing its own no-fly list, which will inevitably be shaped by, and be available to, the Americans and perhaps even others.

As we consider the need to improve our intelligence and law enforcement systems, we must have an open and informed dialogue about what measures truly make us safer while ensuring that our fundamental values and liberties are not sacrificed. The proper forum for such a debate is our legislature.

No-Fly Lists Are Irresponsible

Bypassing this necessary debate in introducing the cleverly named "Passenger protect program" is irresponsible and cavalier, particularly given what we learned from the case of Maher Arar, the Canadian citizen who was rendered to Syria for torture while in transit through New York.

As one of several arguments for discontinuing no-fly lists, the author points to the case of Canadian citizen Maher Arar, who was sent by the United States to Syria for torture as a terrorist—simply because his name appeared on a no-fly list.

This charge is not being made lightly, as the information-sharing protocols and mechanisms, which were criticized by Justice Dennis O'Connor in the Arar inquiry findings, have not been improved or addressed—yet Ottawa [the capital of Canada and center of federal government] is pushing ahead with its list.

Though the government has claimed national security privilege in refusing to confirm or deny this, the Smart Border Declaration and the Security and Prosperity Partnership of North America, as well as intelligence agreements, make it certain that the list will cross-fertilize with U.S., and perhaps even other nations', lists.

Making lengthy watch lists based on subjective and political criteria and then giving the power to add and remove names to agencies that have a vested interest in the national security agenda is akin to asking the fox to guard the hen house.

No-Fly Lists Create a False Sense of Security

Such lists—they will inevitably fill up quickly with "false positives," political dissidents, those whom our friends and neighbours subjectively view as threats—have not yet, as far as the public is aware, caught any terrorists in the U.S.

Indeed, common sense should make us wonder how someone can be too guilty to fly and yet be too innocent to be charged. Should those who pose a threat to our security be kept off our flights, but be free to roam our streets? To make matters worse, real terrorists may not even be placed on the list for fear of tipping them off; no kidding, this is the official U.S. position.

How can such a list provide anything more than a false sense of security while leaving it rife for blacklisting innocent people as well as racial and religious profiling?

Basic Rights Are Threatened

The no-fly list will threaten many basic rights and leave little practical recourse.

Yes, in theory there is the office of reconsideration [the office that reviews security clearances]. But the inability to know whether you are on the list until boarding time, the potential use of secret evidence as well as the use of unreliable and illegally obtained information by

No-Fly List Mistakes

Opponents of no-fly lists say they are riddled with so many errors, they cannot effectively keep Americans safe. The following are just a few people who were either placed on the no-fly list by mistake or were harassed at airports because they share a name with a suspected terrorist.

Sam Adams	Four-year-old boy
Nabih Berri	Head of Lebanese parliament
Daniel Brown	U.S. Marine on his way home from Iraq
David Fathi	Attorney for the American Civil Liberties Union
Asif Iqbal	Management consultant and legal U.S. resident
Yusuf Islam	Former pop singer Cat Stevens
Robert J. Johnson	Surgeon and a former lieutenant colonel in the U.S. Army
Ted Kennedy	U.S. senator from Massachusetts
John Lewis	U.S. representative from Georgia
Patrick Martin	Canadian journalist
Nelson Mandela	Former president of South Africa
James Moore	Emmy-winning news correspondent and author
Evo Morales	President of Bolivia
Walter F. Murphy	Professor at Princeton University
David Nelson	Actor
Kiernan O'Dwyer	Veteran pilot for American Airlines
Jesselyn Radack	Former U.S. Department of Justice ethics advisor
Catherine Stevens	Wife of U.S. senator Ted Stevens
Don Young	U.S. representative from Alaska.

Compiled by the book editor.

foreign sources, will make it near impossible to get off the list in many cases.

This is based on a close review of the U.S. experience as well as the plight of individuals who are already encountering difficulties in flying within Canada without Ottawa even having an official list of our own yet.

The extraterritorial application of U.S. watch lists is already impacting us; how will we fare once we have our own list interacting with, confirming and/or merging with other lists?

No-Fly Lists Increase Racial Profiling

Hasty and ill-considered national security initiatives, which are essentially aimed at managing public perceptions more than they are in really addressing legitimate and manageable security concerns, will not move us forward in the fight to disrupt terrorism. It will only complicate the lives of innocent Canadians and increase the opportunity for religious and racial profiling.

> **FAST FACT**
>
> Many people are mistakenly listed on the no-fly list. These include eighty-nine children, fourteen of whom are under the age of two. The list also includes fourteen of the nineteen September 11 hijackers who have been dead for years.

No matter how vigorously it is denied, racial/religious profiling is too often the reality for a growing number among Canada's Muslim and Arab communities and certainly in the national security context.

The experience of many Canadians who have already been caught up in the web of watch lists, in areas other than flying—be it for opening bank accounts, wiring money, sending courier packages, etc.—does not bode well for the no-fly list.

Bypassing No-Fly Lists Is Easy

And my package? The one that was flagged by "Flight Guardian?"

Well, I drove to a depot close to my office and sent it off—without using an account number and by paying cash.

So much for the security offered by a watch list.

EVALUATING THE AUTHOR'S ARGUMENTS:

Faisal Kutty, the author of this viewpoint, explains how his name was mistakenly placed on a no-fly list after he tried to ship a package to the United States. In your opinion, does the author's personal experience with the no-fly list add credibility to his argument? Or do you think his case is an isolated incident? Explain your position.

Chapter 3

How Should National Security Be Balanced with Civil Liberties?

Items that passengers are prohibited from taking on flights are listed near an airport security checkpoint.

Americans Must Trade Some Freedom for National Security

K.A. Taipale

"In appropriate circumstances and for legitimate purposes government must have access to the information necessary to prevent catastrophic attacks."

In the following viewpoint K.A. Taipale argues that in order to be truly safe, Americans must be prepared to give up some of their freedom. In a free, open society like that of the United States, Taipale says terrorists can take advantage of society's respect for privacy to plot in secrecy. Therefore, says Taipale, it is nearly impossible for authorities to catch terrorists or prevent future attacks without accessing private information. Taipale says the government must have access to data, including personal e-mail accounts, telephone calls, and banking records, and be allowed to spy on suspected criminals. But strict laws dictate how sensitive information can be accessed, and Taipale says some of these laws hamper the government's efforts to isolate terrorists and learn their plans. Taipale concludes it is unreasonable for citizens to expect they can retain absolute privacy and also be protected from terrorists.

Taipale is the founder and executive director of the Center for Advanced Studies in Science and Technology Policy. He is also a senior fellow at the World Policy Institute, where he serves as director of the Global Information Society Project and the Program on Law Enforcement and National Security in the Information Age.

AS YOU READ, CONSIDER THE FOLLOWING QUESTIONS:
1. What amendment does Taipale say allows authorities to investigate legitimately suspicious behavior?
2. According to Taipale, what approach must be taken to identify and stop terrorists before they can attack?
3. What two analytic techniques does Taipale say have been automated to make counterterrorism efforts more effective?

Maintaining privacy expectations that tolerate the planning or commission of catastrophic terrorist acts in secret by denying government access to available information that could help prevent such acts is inherently unreasonable and inconsistent with protecting liberty.

My argument is in three parts: first, potentially catastrophic terrorist attacks require preemptive security strategies; second, modern information technology alters basic assumptions on which many privacy expectations are premised; and, third, certain privacy expectations, especially for electronic data, do not reflect these altered circumstances and are unreasonable.

Expectations About Privacy Are Unreasonable

Privacy expectations are unreasonable when they are premised on simply prohibiting government from using available information. For example, they are unreasonable where they would preclude "connecting the dots" among disparate information sources for counterterrorism purposes by maintaining an artificial "wall" between law enforcement and foreign intelligence activities, or where they would arbitrarily make certain kinds of data—for example, library records—"off limits" for counterterrorism needs.

Privacy expectations are also unreasonable when they are premised exclusively on establishing independently-derived "probable cause" prior to monitoring any electronic records even in those circumstances where the data itself may be the first—or only—available evidence of suspicious behavior, and where it would be wholly consistent with the Fourth Amendment to investigate or monitor such behavior under alternative standards, such as "reasonable suspicion." For example, privacy expectations are unreasonable where they would preclude programmatic monitoring of suspected terrorist communication channels or the routine surveillance of explosives purchases.

To be clear, I am not arguing for a "rebalancing" of security interests over privacy interests but rather proposing the fundamental need to

A U.S. Border Patrol agent searches the vehicle of two women at a search point on a New York highway. The author argues that Americans must give up some freedoms in the interest of security.

rethink how traditional principles, policies and expectations can be applied under these changed circumstances. Indeed, the very metaphor of balancing is itself misleading because security and liberty are dual obligations—not dichotomous rivals to be traded one for the other—and there is no fulcrum at which point the correct amount of security and liberty can be achieved. As [author and intelligence expert] Thomas Powers has pointed out, they are a duality: "In a liberal republic, liberty presupposes security; [and] the point of security is liberty."

Counterterrorism Efforts Require Surveillance

Even the most strident civil libertarians concede that threats with the potential for catastrophic outcomes—for example, nuclear terrorism—require a preemptive approach in which terrorists are identified and stopped before they can act. Preemption requires anticipating and countering potential future events (that is, developing "actionable intelligence").

However, short of clairvoyance, future events can only be anticipated by examining current or past associations or behaviors. Since catastrophic scale terrorist attacks will generally require communications and precursor behaviors likely to be observable or recorded in information systems, counterterrorism intelligence in part requires surveillance (observation) and analysis of data to help identify (anticipate) potentially catastrophic threats so that limited counterterrorism resources can be allocated more successfully.

FAST FACT

Thirty-seven percent of American voters polled in 2009 by Rasmussen Reports believe the U.S. legal system worries too much about protecting individual rights when national security is at stake.

Further, simple "line at the border" perimeter-based defenses are no longer sufficient against terrorists who hide among civilian populations and within normal migration flows to mask their own organization and activities.

Thus, preemptive security strategies necessary to prevent catastrophic attacks inherently involve some form of preventative surveillance and investigation, which will require tempering rigid privacy expectations that are based simply or arbitrarily on keeping information secret.

Information Technology Is Increasingly Useful

Modern information technology has changed fundamental assumptions about information availability and usefulness upon which certain privacy expectations were previously based. Networked digital information systems and distributed search applications have brought an end to the "practical obscurity" that existed when information was difficult to find or access. Now, information routinely available for one purpose is more easily found and retrieved for other uses, like preventing terrorist attacks.

Further, technical means of information acquisition, storage, and processing are capital intensive, not labor or physical space intensive, thus, the economic cost per unit of information has and will continue to decrease. Therefore, whether or not government itself collects information directly, data evidencing associations or behaviors that was previously simply not recorded or stored at all will increasingly exist somewhere, and will be recoverable and subject to analysis where necessary.

In addition, powerful new technologies are being developed to help "make sense of [this] data" [as the author states in another article] by automating certain analytic techniques (including link analysis and pattern recognition). Although critics tend to denigrate their potential, these technologies have already proven themselves in myriad analytic situations previously requiring sophisticated human judgments. These technologies, together with predictive or statistical modeling, are increasingly necessary to allocate limited counterterrorism resources.

Information that previously simply did not exist or was difficult to find, retrieve, or analyze is now increasingly available and useful. Where such information is needed to prevent catastrophic outcomes, government must have authorized access under appropriate procedures. Thus, privacy expectations premised on outdated assumptions that data was simply unavailable or incomprehensible will have to adapt—that is, expectations previously based on the absolute protection afforded by inefficiencies in information availability or processing must now accommodate themselves to more dilute procedural-based protections.

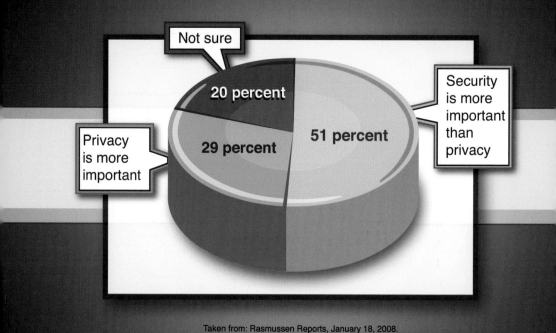

Americans Are Willing to Trade Privacy for Security

A slim majority of Americans believe at least some privacy must be sacrificed in order to achieve national security.

Not sure
20 percent

Security is more important than privacy

51 percent

Privacy is more important

29 percent

Taken from: Rasmussen Reports, January 18, 2008.

Absolute Privacy Is Unrealistic

Privacy means different things to different people but much of the public debate seems to take place within an unexamined mythology of privacy that deifies absolute secrecy and allows no tolerance for even innocuous intrusions or inevitable errors.

Exhorted by a privacy lobby with an institutional fetish for insisting on absolute secrecy over procedural protections (evidenced, for example, by opposition to data retention practices), many privacy expectations are unrealistically inflated based on a presumed privacy entitlement for electronic data that exceeds that demanded by real-world experience or Constitutional requirements.

Further, technology is increasingly burdened with impossible—hence, unreasonable—expectations of proving effectiveness before development and of guaranteeing perfection prior to use. But, opposition to research on the basis that "it might not work" is absurdly shortsighted since the point of research is to determine efficacy. And, demanding perfection—that is, brooking no possibility for any error—before employing technical systems even where they would most certainly provide incremental improvement over existing or alternative methods is, to paraphrase [French author and philosopher] Voltaire, making the perfect the enemy of the better.

Safeguarding Americans from Terrorists

The risk of catastrophic outcomes—including nuclear terrorism—requires the use of preemptive strategies and new technologies against certain threats. Developments in information technology make more information available and more useful. In appropriate circumstances and for legitimate purposes government must have access to the information necessary to prevent catastrophic attacks. To the extent that unrealistic or unreasonable privacy expectations clash with these needs, they will have to be lowered, if only because more flexible procedural protections must be accepted in place of the absolute protections previously afforded by the unavailability or incomprehensibility of data.

EVALUATING THE AUTHOR'S ARGUMENTS:

The author of this viewpoint argues that the government needs access to private information to protect Americans from terrorists. What do you think? Does the government really need this information to track terrorists? If yes, explain your reasoning. If no, suggest another way that the U.S. government might monitor and capture suspected terrorists.

Americans Must Never Trade Freedom for National Security

William F. Jasper

"We are faced with policies, proposals, and legislation that already are dismantling many of our constitutional checks and balances by piecemeal encroachment."

In the following viewpoint William F. Jasper argues that Americans must never trade freedom for national security. He explains how after the terrorist attacks of September 11, 2001, the government created national security policies to fight the "war on terror." However, Jasper contends that many of these policies violate the freedoms and basic rights established by America's Founding Fathers in the U.S. Constitution. For instance, the government has engaged in arbitrary imprisonment and illegal wiretapping, both of which Jasper thinks violate the basic principles on which America was founded. Furthermore, Jasper says that if the government does not protect the rights of its citizens, how can people trust it to protect them from terrorists? Jasper concludes that the U.S. government must find

William F. Jasper, "Real Homeland Security: Accumulation of Power at the Federal Level Is Actually Making America Less Secure. The Answer Is to Return to a Law Enforcement Structure Consistent with Our Constitution," *New American*, April 3, 2006, pp. 10–15. Copyright © 2006 American Opinion Publishing Incorporated. Reproduced by permission.

a way to provide security for the nation while also safeguarding the personal freedoms of all Americans.

Jasper is senior editor at the *New American*. He is also the author of the books *The United Nations Exposed* and *Global Tyranny . . . Step by Step: The United Nations and the Emerging New World Order*.

AS YOU READ, CONSIDER THE FOLLOWING QUESTIONS:

1. According to the author, what act was passed after the September 11, 2001 terrorist attacks that granted the federal government unprecedented power?
2. Whom does the author identify as the "Father of the Constitution"?
3. According to Jasper, what constitutional requirement was whittled away by the administration of George W. Bush and the U.S. Congress?

We must choose, we are told, between security and liberty. If we wish to protect our lives and our nation against terrorists wielding weapons of mass destruction, we must be willing, insist the [George W.] Bush administration and its many allies, to entrust our government with "whatever powers are needed to do the job." And those powers alleged to be so necessary keep growing day by day.

We must be subjected to more searches, screenings, and surveillance, not only at airports but at an ever-increasing number of public venues: court houses, schools, sporting events, bus stations, and train stations. Federal agencies must be empowered to easily and regularly monitor (without warrants) our telephone conversations, e-mail, text messaging, and financial transactions. Local sheriff and police departments must yield their jurisdictions to a national police, i.e., the FBI and the Department of Homeland Security. We must be ready to sacrifice certain sacred rights in the interest of survival: judicial warrants, habeas corpus,[1] a speedy trial, due process, etc. After all, we are at war. And in wartime, it is the patriotic duty of citizens to back their government "all the way," right?

1. A legal action under which people are protected from unlawful imprisonment.

Trading Freedom for Safety

America's Founding Fathers were aware of this argument of necessity. "Safety from external danger is the most powerful director of national conduct," noted [Founding Father] Alexander Hamilton in *The Federalist, No. 8*. He went on to warn: "Even the ardent love of liberty will, after a time, give way to its dictates. The violent destruction of life and property incident to war, the continual effort and alarm attendant on a state of continual danger, will compel nations the most attached to liberty to resort for repose and security to institutions which have a tendency to destroy their civil and political rights. To be more safe, they at length become willing to run the risk of being less free."

To be more safe, are we now more willing "to run the risk of being less free"? Apparently so, according to some polls and indicators. In the immediate aftershock of the September 11, 2001 terrorist attacks, Congress passed a torrent of legislation granting unprecedented new powers to the federal government. One of the first measures passed amidst the panic, anger, and chaos of that period, the so-called Patriot Act, was enacted virtually sight-unseen. Almost no one in Congress had actually read the bill and most did not even have a copy of it. Yet, under pressure to "do something," they overwhelmingly voted it into law.

However, opinion polls and the recent cliffhanger vote on renewal of the Patriot Act suggest that the American public may now be less willing to uncritically accept expanded federal police powers than they were when still reeling from the effects of 9/11. It took months of arm-twisting, pleading, and pressure for the White House to secure passage (by just two votes in the House) on March 7, 2006.

The Constitution Is Threatened by National Security Policies

This is an encouraging sign that many more people are questioning the claims and assumptions underlying the push to gut the Constitution for the professed goal of protecting America against terrorism.

This is not a partisan issue; it is an issue that goes to the very heart of the security and liberty of every single American. The matters at stake are fundamental and urgent. We are faced with policies, proposals, and legislation that already are dismantling many of our constitutional checks and balances by piecemeal encroachment. If the

"Sacrificing Privacy," cartoon by Keefe, *The Denver Post,* November 16, 2002. Copyright © 2002 Keefe, The Denver Post, and PoliticalCartoons.com.

process is not stopped and rolled back, it will eventually obliterate them entirely.

We do not know precisely where the point of no return is in this process. No one does—until it's too late. But we can recognize the process and the signposts. As James Madison, the "Father of the Constitution," observed: "Since the general civilization of mankind, I believe there are more instances of the abridgement of the freedom of the people by gradual and silent encroachments of those in power than by violent and sudden usurpations."

We Are Not Safer from Terrorism

There is no question that Americans are becoming "less free," but in the trade-off, are we not at least becoming "more safe" from terrorism? Unfortunately, no. In fact, under George Bush, as under Bill

Clinton, we are sacrificing both freedom and safety in a so-called "war on terror." In the name of security, we are allowing America to be transformed from a limited constitutional republic into a repressive police state. Again, we should heed Mr. Madison, who observed in *The Federalist, No. 47*, "The accumulation of all powers, legislative, executive, and judiciary, in the same hands . . . may justly be pronounced the very definition of tyranny."

Contrary to current popular wisdom, much of the federal program being advanced under the "war on terror" banner cannot pass muster on either constitutional or practical grounds. It is essential for us to realize that maintaining our constitutional structure and principles is not merely a legal nicety but an absolute necessity if we are to be governed by the "rule of law" rather than dictatorial whim. But as a practical matter, our constitutional system also provides protections against terrorism that a centralized behemoth would not have.

As the Founders pointed out, we have not just a republic, but a "compound republic," with powers distributed not only among the legislative, executive, and judicial branches, but even more importantly, between the federal, state, and local governments. This arrangement not only provides an essential safeguard against dangerous concentration of power in government, but also provides a multi-layered defense-in-depth that is vital to defending America against terrorism. . . .

Americans' Basic Rights Are in Jeopardy

Some of [President Bush's] most egregious and persistent assaults concern arbitrary imprisonment without charge and the insistence that even American citizens may not have the benefit of their most ancient protection of habeas corpus, which Alexander Hamilton called "the BULWARK of the British Constitution." (Emphasis in original.)

Writing in *The Federalist, No. 84*, Hamilton notes that ex post facto laws "and the practice of arbitrary imprisonments, have been, in all ages, the favorite and most formidable instruments of tyranny." He

The author cites Alexander Hamilton's writings in The Federalist Papers *to make his point that Americans need the protections afforded under habeas corpus to protect themselves from unlawful imprisonment.*

quotes [noted English jurist William] Blackstone, who remarks: "To bereave a man of life, or by violence to confiscate his estate, without accusation or trial, would be so gross and notorious an act of despotism, as must at once convey the alarm of tyranny throughout the whole nation; but confinement of the person, by secretly hurrying him to jail, where his sufferings are unknown or forgotten, is a less public, a less striking, and therefore a more dangerous engine of arbitrary government."

When President Bush and Attorney General [John] Ashcroft sent the first draft of the Patriot Act to the House Judiciary Committee, it contained a section entitled "Suspension of the Writ of Habeas Corpus." This was such an outrageous proposal that it was struck from the text. However, what couldn't be obtained in one outright usurpation is being obtained through gradual encroachment.

Similarly, the administration and its congressional lackeys have been whittling away the constitutional requirement of judicial warrants for search and seizure, claiming wide-ranging authority to wiretap phones, faxes, e-mail—virtually all electronic communications. Quoting [French philosopher, the Baron de] Montesquieu, Hamilton writes in *The Federalist, No. 78*, "For I agree, that 'there is no liberty, if the power of judging be not separated from the legislative and executive powers.'" Resist efforts to undermine this important separation, Hamilton cautioned, "as no man can be sure that he may not be tomorrow the victim of a spirit of injustice, by which he may become gainer today." . . .

Civil Liberties Must Be Protected

We must reestablish the multi-layered defense-in-depth consonant with our security needs as well as the constitutional principles provided by the Founders. That means first and foremost keeping our local police forces local and independent of federal funding and controls. Local and state police should cooperate with federal law enforcement authorities in proper areas, including terrorism—as they have traditionally done—but they must not become mere administrative units of a federal police leviathan.

The federal legislative, executive, and judicial functions must be kept in their respective spheres, and efforts to combine or encroach must be adamantly opposed. Even more important, the extensive powers at the state and local levels must be protected against federal usurpation. Or, as Mr. Madison succinctly put it, "Ambition must be made to counteract ambition." And that, at this very critical juncture in the history of our battered republic, is a very ambitious and worthy goal indeed.

EVALUATING THE AUTHOR'S ARGUMENTS:

In this viewpoint William Jasper includes several quotes from America's Founding Fathers to prove his point that Americans' freedoms are threatened by current national security policies. In your opinion, did these quotes help prove his point? Why or why not?

Americans Do Not Have to Choose Between Freedom and Security

Doris O. Matsui

"Our national discourse wrongly assumes that liberty and security are mutually exclusive ideals."

Doris O. Matsui argues in the following viewpoint that Americans do not have to choose between freedom and security. She explains that national security and personal liberty actually go hand in hand. She discusses a piece of legislation—the RESTORE Act—which attempts to balance these two ideals. Matsui explains that this act will protect Americans from potential terrorist attacks and at the same time ensure that the ideals upon which the country was founded are maintained. Americans will not have to fear that their personal and private information will be exploited and can rest assured that officials will gather intelligence legally. For example, RESTORE would require a war-

Doris O. Matsui, "Liberty and Security Are Not Mutually Exclusive," *San Francisco Chronicle*, October 31, 2007. Reproduced by permission of the author.

rant to be obtained before authorities conduct surveillance on an American citizen. But it would also allow authorities to pursue potential terrorist suspects using the latest data-mining technologies. Matsui concludes that Americans need not sacrifice their personal freedoms for the sake of national security—laws like RESTORE can offer them both.

Matsui is a Democrat in the U.S. House of Representatives, representing California's Fifth Congressional District.

AS YOU READ, CONSIDER THE FOLLOWING QUESTIONS:
1. What does the author criticize as being a "dramatic and emotional appeal"?
2. According to Matsui, what amendment to the U.S. Constitution will be protected by the RESTORE Act?
3. What act does Matsui say is improved under the new RESTORE Act?

At times, our national discourse wrongly assumes that liberty and security are mutually exclusive ideals. In fact, our liberty is a crucial component of our national security. Soon, the House [of Representatives] will consider the RESTORE Act, a piece of legislation that maintains a balance between these two ideals. The RESTORE Act is the result of intense study, having been examined from every possible angle by some of our nation's prominent leaders. Through reasoned logic, it accomplishes what previous laws could not: It responsibly seeks to protect Americans from another terrorist attack while still preserving our fundamental, core values.

Both National Security and Civil Liberties Must Be Preserved

We are at a point in our country's history where people are acutely aware of national security, and the imperative to conduct effective counterterrorism operations. No American citizen, no elected official and no government agency can deny that we must pay close attention to our security needs. At the same time, our devotion to our civil liberties is what separates our country and signifies our leadership in the international community.

Some government officials and members of Congress have spoken in the media and on the House floor using incendiary language, hoping that it will resonate with the American people and cause us to change our path: saying that "people will die" and that we cannot "impede surveillance of [terrorist leader] Osama bin Laden."

No upstanding citizen of this country wants to see Americans die . . . or hinder the process of bringing Osama bin Laden to justice. But I refuse to respond to this dramatic and emotional appeal, and instead call on the American people and my colleagues in Congress to examine the issue from a well-reasoned position and an eye to the preservation of our national security and civil liberties.

Changing Technology Requires Flexibility

As lawmakers, we must have the strength and moral fiber to not give in to the rhetoric of fear, but to explore the avenues that will bolster our national security, provide our law enforcement personnel with the tools they need to effectively do their jobs, and preserve our civil liberties and way of life. Citizenship in the United States must stand for something.

FAST FACT

In a 2008 Rasmussen Reports telephone survey, 69 percent of voters agreed that telecommunications companies can turn over customer records as long as the government has obtained a search warrant.

In testimony before the Senate, Director of National Intelligence Mike McConnell asked for three things: streamlining the FISA [Foreign Intelligence Surveillance Act] process, flexibility in pursuing foreign targets and immunity for telecommunications companies who handed over information to the government.

In the RESTORE Act, Congress has developed policy that grants this flexibility and allows for an improved procedure, while recognizing changing technology and trends. It also grants broad authority to our security agencies to pursue foreign targets, while still affording Fourth

The author says that the RESTORE Act of 2007 balances the need to protect American citizens' rights while still using the latest data-mining technologies to protect American lives.

Amendment protection to American citizens. The RESTORE Act grants broad latitude in pursuing individuals outside of the United States but requires that for surveillance of an American citizen to be conducted, a warrant must be obtained.

Intelligence Procedures Must Follow the Law

In fact, the RESTORE Act improves upon the Protect Americans Act by providing clarity to our intelligence agencies, which actually helps in surveillance activities and terrorism prevention. Without clear guidelines of permissible behavior and procedure, law enforcement agents will err on the side of caution. Clarity allows them to confidently conduct surveillance and counterterrorism efforts without fear of persecution. Having a strong legal footing ensures that prosecutions of terrorists and other criminals will not be jeopardized.

The legislation that we are pursuing in Congress is focused on protecting Americans from terrorist attacks. But the fact of the matter is that we must proceed with due diligence and with full appreciation of the effects such legislation will have on our way of life.

As former deputy attorney general James B. Comey said in an address to the National Security Agency in May 2005, "It takes an appreciation of the damage that will flow from an unjustified 'yes.' It takes an understanding that, in the long-run, intelligence under law is the only sustainable intelligence in this country." . . .

Civil Liberties Must Be Protected

And that is where we must take a stand, and not treat the law or our Constitutional rights lightly. Brave men and women have died to protect the civil liberties and values that we hold most dear. We cannot and should not lightly brush their sacrifices aside; instead we must honor their memories by taking responsible action to ensure our nation's security. As the late Milton Friedman, an economist and Nobel Laureate, said, "Eternal vigilance is required and there have to be people who step up to the plate, who believe in liberty, and who are willing to fight for it."

EVALUATING THE AUTHOR'S ARGUMENTS:

In this viewpoint Matsui states that it is a fundamental right for all Americans to live in a safe and secure nation while also maintaining their privacy and personal freedoms. What do you think? Is it possible to balance both security and liberty equally? Would there ever be an instance where this might not be possible? Explain your position.

National ID Cards Violate Privacy

Jim Harper

"The state should reject the privacy and security nightmare known as the REAL ID Act."

In the following viewpoint Jim Harper argues that national identification cards violate the privacy of American citizens. Although the U.S. government claims that a national ID database will enhance national security, Harper disagrees. He says the creation of such cards requires sensitive information to be compiled into one large database. Harper argues that this system could be hacked, compromising hundreds of thousands of people's personal information. Furthermore, he predicts that terrorists and criminals will find a way to keep their information out of the system anyway, thereby rendering it useless for catching terrorists. Harper warns that national ID cards are nothing more than a way for the federal government to monitor the actions of law-abiding citizens. He concludes that the proposal to create a national identification card violates the civil liberties of the American people.

Harper is director of information policy studies at the Cato Institute, a nonprofit public policy research institute.

AS YOU READ, CONSIDER THE FOLLOWING QUESTIONS:
1. How many states does Harper say passed laws in 2007 that oppose the federal government's national identification program?
2. What two types of documents does Harper say would go in a national ID database?
3. According to Harper, how many states complied with the REAL ID law by the May 11, 2008 deadline?

L ast year [2007] seventeen states passed legislation objecting to the REAL ID Act, a massive national identification program the federal government is trying to foist on the American people through their states' driver licensing systems. Virginia may soon join those states in the REAL ID rebellion. Today, [February 7, 2008], the Virginia Senate's Transportation Committee will consider a bill to reject the unfunded mandates in the REAL ID Act.

Under the bill, the [Virginia] Department of Health's Office of Vital Records and the Department of Motor Vehicles would develop and implement a plan to provide Virginia residents with appropriate identity verification. This would let Virginians avoid the national ID system, a network of government databases containing basic identity information, including scanned copies of Social Security cards and birth certificates.

The Government Will Use National ID Cards to Control Citizens

With so many states on record opposing REAL ID, the feds have been shifting through numerous stories trying to justify their national ID. First, they said it was a national security tool. But by now everyone realizes how easy it would be for criminal organizations and terrorists to avoid or defeat a national ID system.

Then REAL ID became a way to control illegal immigration. But it has the same defects here too. Illegal immigrants will use a mix of forgery, fraud, and corruption at any motor vehicles bureau in the country to get around REAL ID. Driving illegal immigrants further into criminality deepens the problem rather than fixing it. And should law-abiding American citizens really have to carry a national ID to get at illegal immigrants? Just who is the criminal here?

Next, we were told that having a national ID was about identity fraud. But putting our personal information, Social Security Numbers, and basic identity documents like birth certificates into a nationwide string of government databases is a recipe for more identity theft, not less.

Britain's home secretary, Jaqui Smith, displays a new UK identity card in 2008. The author says a like measure is not useful in the United States because terrorists will find ways to avoid being identified.

When the Department of Homeland Security [DHS] came out with the final REAL ID regulations [in January 2008], a top official threw the department's final Hail Mary [pass; i.e., a last desperate attempt], suggesting that REAL ID could be used to control access to cold medicine. That's right: cold medicine. The lesson? Once a national ID system is in place, the federal government will use it for tighter and tighter control of every American.

National ID Cards Cannot Protect Privacy

The DHS has admitted that not a single state will comply with the REAL ID law by the May 11, 2008 deadline. Even today, nobody knows how to build a massive database system that protects Americans' privacy and data security. So the department is giving states extensions until the end of 2009, just for the asking. It is also threatening to send air travelers to secondary search at airports if their states haven't applied for those extensions and kissed the DHS ring [i.e., showed obedience].

FAST FACT

According to Harvard University, as of May 11, 2008—the deadline for implementing the REAL ID system—not a single state was in compliance with the new law. In fact, nineteen states had rejected the national ID program, saying the IDs violate privacy.

Why the brinksmanship? Here's one reason: The top DHS officials involved in REAL ID will be leaving their jobs by the end of the year. A new administration takes over in January 2009, and they intend to be ensconced all around Washington, D.C. in lobbying and consulting jobs by then. Their prospects rise if they have a program to lobby for, and they want to score a victory.

Politics, Not Security

REAL ID isn't about national security. It isn't about illegal immigration. It isn't about identity fraud, or even cold medicine. It's about Washington politics. Federal bureaucrats want to coerce states like Virginia into building a multi-billion dollar system for identifying, tracking, and controlling law-abiding citizens.

Knowing how the Washington bureaucracy works against our nation's founding principles of limited government and individual liberty, conservative leaders across the country have joined with others to call the Department of Homeland Security's bluff. With enough states saying "Hell No" to the REAL ID mandate, the feds will back

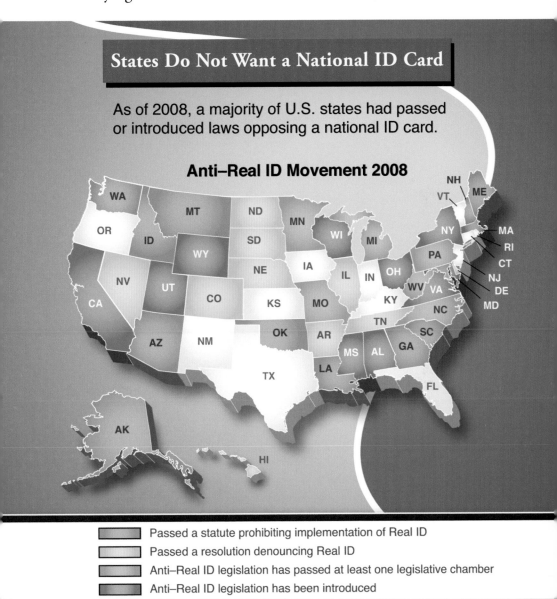

States Do Not Want a National ID Card

As of 2008, a majority of U.S. states had passed or introduced laws opposing a national ID card.

Anti–Real ID Movement 2008

Passed a statute prohibiting implementation of Real ID

Passed a resolution denouncing Real ID

Anti–Real ID legislation has passed at least one legislative chamber

Anti–Real ID legislation has been introduced

Taken from: www.realnightmare.org and the American Civil Liberties Union, 2009.

down from their threat to make air travel inconvenient. The airline industry will be up on Capitol Hill faster than you can say "You are now free to move about the country." Congress will back the DHS off.

The country will be the better for it if the revolutionary spirit revives in the Old Dominion [Virginia]. The state should reject the privacy and security nightmare known as the REAL ID Act.

EVALUATING THE AUTHOR'S ARGUMENTS:

In the viewpoint you just read, Jim Harper uses history, facts, and examples to make his point that Americans' privacy would be violated if they were required to carry national ID Cards. He does not, however, use any quotations to support his point. If you rewrote the article and inserted quotations, what authorities might you quote from? Where would you place these quotations to bolster the points Harper makes?

Viewpoint
5

National ID Cards Do Not Violate Privacy

Froma Harrop

"A secure form of identification is the simplest and least discriminatory tool for preventing terrorist attacks."

Froma Harrop argues in the following viewpoint that national identification cards do not violate personal privacy. She explains that national ID cards would ensure that birth certificates and passports are genuine and would prevent terrorists and other criminals from making fake IDs. Harrop says opponents of such cards are paranoid to think that national ID cards will violate Americans' privacy by making personal information available to the government. Rather, Harrop asserts that such cards would be well secured and would not contain much more information than already exists on driver's licenses. She concludes that national ID cards are a secure way to protect Americans from terrorists and other criminals who illegally obtain IDs and thus are an important part of national security.

Harrop is a columnist for the *Providence (RI) Journal.* Her column is syndicated in over two hundred newspapers, including the *Seattle Times* and *Newsday.*

Froma Harrop, "Overwrought Opposition to a Secure National ID Card," *Seattle Times*, February 23, 2007. Reproduced by permission of the author.

AS YOU READ, CONSIDER THE FOLLOWING QUESTIONS:

1. In what year did Congress pass the "Real ID" law?
2. What states does Harrop say have in some way expressed objections to the Real ID law?
3. According to Harrop, the bar code on a national ID card would be virtually the same as the bar code on what common form of identification?

Airport security lets us onto an airplane based on our state-issued driver's license. So it made sense for the 9-11 commission to recommend creating federal standards to ensure that the people flashing their driver's licenses are who they say they are.

In 2005, Congress passed the "Real ID" law to achieve just that. Though a secure form of identification is the simplest and least discriminatory tool for preventing terrorist attacks, it has lots of enemies.

Missouri state Rep. Jim Guest, a Republican, has called Real ID "a frontal assault on the freedom of Americans." It's frankly hard to see what freedom is under assault other than the freedom to lie on your driver's license. Perhaps Guest can elaborate.

FAST FACT

In a Pew Research Center poll conducted a week after the September 11 terrorist attacks, 70 percent of respondents supported a national ID card that could be shown to authorities on demand.

Real ID Is Not Meant to Control Americans

Such scare talk has addled brains in places like Maine, where the Legislature recently voted to demand that Congress repeal the Real ID law. Washington, Arizona, Georgia, Oklahoma and several other states are in various stages of revolt—and expressing shock at a form of ID that's routine in the liberal democracies of Europe.

Cheap-labor advocates don't like Real ID because states would have to verify that the license applicant is in this country legally. Supporters

U.S. senator Susan Collins of Maine speaks to the press in March 2007 about the Department of Homeland Security's decision to delay implementation of the Real ID Act. The author disagrees with the decision.

of illegal immigrants feel likewise. The crazy fringes, meanwhile, portray a secure driver's license as the federal jackboots' weapon to control us all. Others just play the nut-job out of political expediency.

The 1986 immigration reform bill, which granted amnesty to more than 3 million illegal immigrants, originally contained a provision for a national ID system. During the debate, Rep. Edward Roybal, a Democrat from California, got up and warned, "We may face the danger of ending up like Nazi Germany." The ID provision was scratched off the bill.

These dramatics amazed the Rev. Theodore Hesburgh, former president of the University of Notre Dame and chairman of a committee on immigration in the '80s. "There were all kinds of phony excuses," he told the *Washington Post*.

National ID Cards Are Secure

Under Real ID, states must check that the documents presented for getting a driver's license—such as a birth certificate or passport—are genuine. The licenses must also contain a digital photo and some form of biometric data, such as a thumbprint. Driver's licenses from states that don't comply would not be acceptable proof of identification at airports or federal buildings.

Some privacy advocates insist that Real ID would foster more identification theft. They are misinformed. It would do the opposite by cutting down on the use of counterfeit IDs.

In case you haven't noticed, there are no deep, dark personal secrets on your driver's license. With Real ID, the stuff on the face of the license would be pretty much what's there now. And that "sinister" bar code would contain the same information seen on the card. It doesn't lead to your bank account or love letters.

Identity Cards Will Help Keep Americans Safe

What on Earth could Maine lawmakers have been thinking—especially after having heard the testimony of a worker at their department of motor vehicles? Jennifer Pease explained that it was official policy to

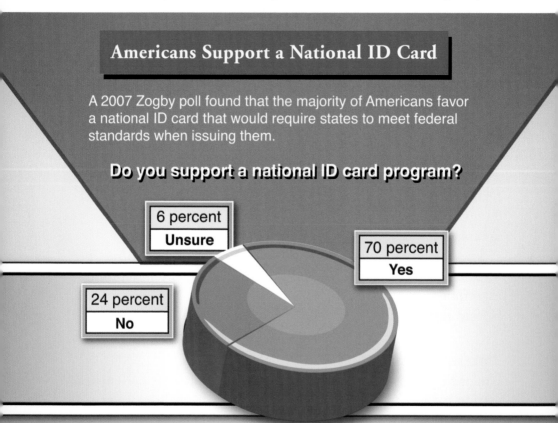

Americans Support a National ID Card

A 2007 Zogby poll found that the majority of Americans favor a national ID card that would require states to meet federal standards when issuing them.

Do you support a national ID card program?

6 percent
Unsure

70 percent
Yes

24 percent
No

Taken from: Zogby International, April 22, 2007.

ignore expiration dates on passports and visas and to knowingly issue licenses and ID cards to illegal immigrants. One applicant was an Egyptian national from New York who had no intention of living in Maine and was facing deportation proceedings. His license was mailed to a post-office box in Portland.

When you have left-wingers, right-wingers, foes and friends of illegal immigrants, libertarians, the U.S. Chamber of Commerce, several church leaders and the American Civil Liberties Union all lined up against a secure identity card, you know it's going to be tough sledding.

That, however, does not make it a bad idea.

EVALUATING THE AUTHOR'S ARGUMENTS:

In the viewpoint you just read, Froma Harrop argues that national ID cards are a secure and private way to achieve national security. What do you think? Would you mind if your private information was contained in a national identity card? Would this feel different to you than having a driver's license? Why or why not?

Newspapers Should Not Report Stories That Compromise National Security

Heather Mac Donald

"No classified secret necessary to fight terrorism is safe once the [New York] Times hears of it."

In the following viewpoint Heather Mac Donald argues that newspapers should not report stories that compromise national security. She says when newspapers reveal secret programs or tactics for capturing terrorists, terrorists are able to use the information to evade capture. Such stories can seriously undermine U.S. efforts to fight terrorism and can put the lives of counterterrorism officials at risk. No matter how interesting or newsworthy a story is, Mac Donald thinks newspapers should not print it if it compromises U.S. security. Newspapers have a moral obligation to protect the security of the United States, and Mac

Donald thinks they should sacrifice a good story if it will help protect their country. Mac Donald concludes that national security secrets should never be revealed in the nation's newspapers.

Mac Donald is a contributing editor to the Manhattan Institute's *City Journal*, an urban policy magazine. She is the author of three books, including *The Immigration Solution: A Better Plan than Today's*.

AS YOU READ, CONSIDER THE FOLLOWING QUESTIONS:
1. What was the headline of a *New York Times* story that Mac Donald says blew the cover on a secret government program to locate terrorist financing networks?
2. What Belgian clearinghouse did the *New York Times* expose classified information about in one of its stories, according to Mac Donald?
3. What does the word "paranoia" mean in the context of the viewpoint?

By now it's undeniable: The *New York Times* is a national security threat. So drunk is it on its own power and so antagonistic to the [George W.] Bush administration that it will expose every classified antiterror program it finds out about, no matter how legal the program, how carefully crafted to safeguard civil liberties, or how vital to protecting American lives.

The *Times*'s latest revelation of a national security secret appeared on last Friday's [June 30, 2006] front page—where no al Qaeda operative could possibly miss it. Under the deliberately sensational headline, "Bank Data Sifted in Secret by U.S. to Block Terror," the *Times* blows the cover on a highly targeted program to locate terrorist financing networks. According to the report, since 9/11, the Bush administration has obtained information about terror suspects' international financial transactions from a Belgian clearinghouse of international money transfers.

National Security Programs Are Legal
The procedure for obtaining that information could not be more solicitous of privacy and the rule of law: Agents are only allowed to seek

information based on intelligence tying specific individuals to al Qaeda; they must document the intelligence behind every search request and maintain an electronic record of every search; and, in an inspired civil liberties innovation that would undoubtedly garner kudos from the *Times* had a Democratic administration devised it, a board of independent auditors from banks reviews the subpoena requests to make sure that only terror suspects' transactions are traced. Any use of the data for criminal investigations into drug trafficking, say, or tax fraud is banned. The administration briefed congressional leaders and the 9/11 Commission about the system.

There is nothing about this program that exudes even a whiff of illegality. The Supreme Court has squarely held that bank records are not constitutionally protected private information. The government may obtain them without seeking a warrant from a court, because the bank depositor has already revealed his transactions to his bank—or, in the case of the present program, to a whole slew of banks that participate in the complicated international wire transfers overseen by the Belgian clearinghouse known as the Society for Worldwide Interbank Financial Telecommunication, or Swift. To get specific information about individual terror suspects, intelligence agents prepare an administrative subpoena, which is issued after extensive internal agency review. The government does not monitor a terror suspect's international wire transfers in real time; the records of his transactions are delivered weeks later. And Americans' routine financial transactions, such as ATM withdrawals or domestic banking, lie completely outside of the Swift database.

Newspapers Expose Classified Information

The administration strongly urged the *New York Times* not to expose this classified program, and for good reason. According to the *Times* itself, the program has proven vital in hunting down international killers. The Indonesian terrorist Hambali, who orchestrated the Bali resort bombings in 2002, was captured through the Swift program; a Brooklyn man who laundered $200,000 for al Qaeda through a Karachi bank was tracked via the program. The *Wall Street Journal* adds that the July 7, 2005, London subway bombings were fruitfully investigated through the Swift initiative and that a facilitator of Iraqi terrorism has been apprehended because of it.

A coterie of former and current Democratic and Republican leaders also begged the *Times* not to jeopardize this highly successful counterterrorism program, but the *Times* knew better. In a smug prepared statement, executive editor Bill Keller emotes: "We remain convinced that the administration's extraordinary access to this vast repository of international financial data, however carefully targeted use of it may be, is a matter of public interest."

Now that the *Times* has blown the cover on this terror-tracking initiative, sophisticated terrorists will figure out how to evade it, according to the Treasury's top counterterrorism official, Stuart Levey, speaking to the *Wall Street Journal*. The lifeblood of international terrorism—cash—will once again flow undetected.

The United States Cannot Fight Terrorism if National Security Secrets Are Revealed

The bottom line is this: No classified secret necessary to fight terrorism is safe once the *Times* hears of it, at least as long as the Bush administration is in power. The *Times* justifies its national security breaches by the

The author cites the New York Times's *exposure of the classified Society for Worldwide Interbank Financial Telecommunication (SWIFT) program as an example of how freedom of the press can undermine national security efforts.*

mere hypothetical possibility of abuse—without providing any evidence that this financial tracking program, or any other classified antiterror initiative that it has revealed, actually has been abused. To the contrary, the paper reports that one employee was taken off the Swift program for conducting a search that did not obviously fall within the guidelines.

The truth the *Times* evades is that while every power, public or private, can be misused, the mere possibility of abuse does not mean that a necessary power should be discarded. Instead, the rational response is to create checks that minimize the risk of abuse. Under the *Times*'s otherworldly logic, the United States might be better off with no government at all, because governmental power can be abused. It should not have newspapers, because the power of the press can be abused to harm the national interest (as the *Times* so amply demonstrates). Police forces should be disbanded, because police officers can overstep their authority. National security wiretaps? Heavens! Expose all of them.

Newspapers Are Paranoid

The *Times* implies a second reason it ignored the government's fervent requests to protect the program's secrecy: Large databases were involved. The *Times* has an attack of the vapors whenever evidence of terrorist planning is found in databases, reasoning that any program to harvest that evidence is a privacy threat and should be exposed. Such logic, if taken seriously, would mean an end to all computerized investigations and would create an impregnable shield to terrorist activity in cyberspace. Anything a terrorist does that is recorded by computers will by its very nature be interspersed among records of millions if not billions or trillions of innocent transactions by unrelated parties. That fact alone should not disable the government from seeking the evidence; it merely means that the government should follow existing procedures governing the collection of evidence—as, in the case of the Swift program, it has.

The paranoia of the *New York Times*'s editors really has reached astonishing levels. When you think about it, virtually *every* piece of evidence ever gathered in criminal or national security cases is embedded in harmless activity. On the *Times*'s theory, police officers should not walk beats looking for criminal activity, because they are observing innocent passersby as well.

Innovative Security Programs Are Needed

The *Times* offers a third justification for its reckless breach of national security: "The program . . . is a significant departure from typical practice in how the government acquires Americans' financial records." Indeed. And 9/11 marked a significant departure from most Americans' experience of jet travel. The hijackings revealed unmistakably the need for innovative intelligence programs to disrupt future attacks. By the *Times*'s hidebound ethic, however, anything new that the Bush administration does to protect the public is suspect and must be revealed. Needless to add, this prejudice against innovation will not prevent the *Times* from raising hell about Bush administration incompetence if the country is attacked again, just as the *Times* railed against the administration for "failing to connect the dots" before 9/11—a failure caused in large part by unnecessary civil libertarian restraints on fully lawful powers.

The *Times*'s ritual invocation of the "public interest" cannot disguise the weakness of their argument for revealing this highly successful antiterror program. Its editors seem aware of this, and hence try to link this program to the more legitimately controversial NSA [National Security Agency] wiretapping program that was revealed (by the same reporters— Eric Lichtblau and James Risen) last December [2005], also in defiance of administration requests. Though acknowledging in passing that the Swift program is in fact separate from the wiretapping program, the *Times* links them on the grounds that both "grew out of the Bush administration's desire to exploit technological tools to prevent another terrorist strike." The revelation of the NSA program has "provoked fierce public debate and spurred lawsuits," the *Times* notes with self-satisfaction, and thus, by implication, the Swift program should, too. Do they seriously believe the U.S. government should *not* exploit technological tools in the war on terror?

Terrorists Manipulate the Media

Al Qaeda has long worked to manipulate the media in its favor. It can disband that operation now, knowing that, unbidden, America's most powerful newspaper is looking out for its interests.

EVALUATING THE AUTHOR'S ARGUMENTS:

In this viewpoint Heather Mac Donald accuses the *New York Times* of publishing stories that compromise America's national security. What role do you think a newspaper should have during periods of heightened security? Do Americans need to know the kinds of stories the *New York Times* has reported, or does the publication of such stories compromise security? Explain what kinds of stories you think newspapers should publish regarding national security.

Newspapers Have an Obligation to Report All Stories

Dante Chinni

> "The press was not meant only to be a megaphone for those in power . . . it was to be a monitor of power."

Dante Chinni argues in the following viewpoint that newspapers have an obligation to report all stories, even ones about sensitive issues like national security. Many newspapers have come under criticism for publishing what the government says is classified national security information. But Chinni suggests that newspapers keep Americans critically informed about the actions of government officials. Without newspaper stories, citizens would not know what America's leaders are really up to and whether they are behaving constitutionally. Chinni says it is the newspapers' job to help keep the government in check and thus help keep Americans safe from tyrannical rule. As long as newspapers are careful about the way they present national security information, Chinni sees no problem with reporting stories that are of concern to the American people.

Dante Chinni, "National Security vs. Freedom of the Press: The Media Must Monitor the Powerful, Not Just Serve as Their Mouthpiece," *Christian Science Monitor*, May 23, 2006. Copyright © 2006 The Christian Science Publishing Society. All rights reserved. Reproduced by permission from *Christian Science Monitor*, (www.csmonitor.com).

Chinni concludes that freedom of the press is an important principle and must be honored at all costs.

Chinni is a political columnist for the *Christian Science Monitor* and a Washington, D.C., magazine writer. He has written for the *Washington Post Magazine*, the *Economist*, the *New Republic*, and the *Columbia Journalism Review*.

AS YOU READ, CONSIDER THE FOLLOWING QUESTIONS:

1. What news outlet does Chinni say received a warning that two of its reporters' phone calls were being wiretapped?
2. According to Chinni, what news story did the *New York Times* wait to release for over a year?
3. What was America's Founding Fathers' primary concern, according to Chinni?

Most everyone loves a whistle-blower. When there are shady dealings or bureaucratic bunglings, often it is the whistle-blower, the guy or gal on the inside with the unfailing moral compass who simply can't bear it anymore, who comes out the hero.

Sherron Watkins, Enron's famous insider,[1] not only exposed that company's accounting scams, her testimony before Congress made her a star. She was one of *Time* magazine's people of the year in 2002. And she later went on to become a well-known consultant and public speaker.

How can you not love someone like Ms. Watkins who puts it all on the line for truth, justice, and the common good—unless, of course, you're Ken Lay?[2]

Freedom of the Press May Be in Jeopardy

But it's not always that clean in the age of the "war on terror." Truth may be clear in many cases, but the common good is not always defined the same way by every person. And that has placed the news media in an awkward situation.

1. Enron was a corporation involved in a substantial financial scandal in 2001.
2. Lay was found guilty of conspiracy and fraud in the Enron scandal.

Last week [May 2006], ABC News reported that two of its correspondents were warned by a source, "It's time for you to get some new cellphones, quick." The implication was that the reporters' phone calls were being tracked by government so it could learn who their confidential sources were.

The FBI later acknowledged that, in cases where it was taking "logical investigative steps to determine if a criminal act was committed by a government employee by the unauthorized release of classified information," there are times when "the records of a private person are sought"—including a journalist's—through an established legal process.

[In May 2006], Attorney General Alberto Gonzales said laws on the books seem to indicate that journalists could be prosecuted for publishing classified information.

In May 2006 U.S. attorney general Alberto Gonzales responds to an ABC News story asserting that journalists could be prosecuted for publishing classified information.

The Media Are Careful with National Security Information

Some undoubtedly cheer that kind of thinking. Anything to keep us safe. And the questions this scenario raises are obvious. Are these whistle-blowers heroes or traitors? And, when the media publishes and airs their allegations, are they complicit in bringing justice or aiding the enemy?

It's sad, but for some this question has been reduced to just another subargument in the nation's all-consuming blue- versus red-America political debate. President [George W.] Bush's supporters see turncoats in the press reports and his detractors see warriors for truth. But before everyone suits up in his and her red and blue jerseys, they should consider what's at stake.

> **FAST FACT**
>
> According to a 2007 Pew Research Center survey, 42 percent of those surveyed believed that newspapers that leaked national security stories were serving the public's interest by providing Americans with information they should have.

First, the media doesn't treat national security leaks the way they do speculation about cabinet hirings and firings. The *New York Times* sat on its National Security Agency wiretap story for a year before running it in December [2005]. Despite multiple leaks of CIA official Valerie Plame's name to the press, only one journalist ran with it—and that's noteworthy.

The Media Serve to Monitor Power

Pressure to be first with news has increased in recent years, but news outlets still have an extremely high standard for anything concerning the nation's safety and the lives of its people. Any information they ultimately choose to publish or air has almost always gone though rigorous vetting. And the value of making the information public has been seriously contemplated and weighed. Second, whatever anyone says, the debate over stopping government leakers is not about politics; it is about government power. Whistle-blowers and the media outlets they ultimately talk to serve a vital role—one that was imag-

Americans Want Freedom of the Press

Americans have gained an increasing appreciation of freedom of the press since 1991. More Americans than ever believe the news media should be able to report stories that are of importance to Americans, and the government should not be able to censor news stories in the name of national security.

Which is more important to you—that the government be able to censor news stories it feels threaten national security OR that the news media be able to report stories they feel are in the national interest?

	Government Able to Censor	News Media Able to Report	Both Equal	Unsure
February 1–5, 2006	34	56	5	5
February 2003	42	50	2	6
November 2001	53	39	4	4
March 1991	58	32	5	5
	Percentage of Poll Respondents			

Taken from: Pew Research Center for the People & the Press Survey, February 1–5, 2006.

ined by the founders of this country. The press was not meant only to be a megaphone for those in power—a means to keep people informed of what they were doing—it was to be a monitor of power.

Newspapers Are a Place of Last Resort

Are there risks to this approach where national security is concerned? To some extent, yes. The media's concern is not a guarantee. But that risk has to be taken if the Founding Fathers' primary concern, the fear of government tyranny, is to be honored. There has to be a place of last resort for government workers to go when they feel their employer is in the wrong.

Ultimately, the question is, will the nation's security come at the expense of the nation's bedrock principles? And the respective sides in the great blue- versus red-America debate should look beyond the present before they get too vociferous in their arguments. They may soon find that those arguments are changing.

After all, Republicans won't be in charge of the White House forever, and Democrats probably won't always be the ones rejoicing when whistle-blowers come forward.

EVALUATING THE AUTHOR'S ARGUMENTS:

In this viewpoint Dante Chinni explains that newspapers and other media must report all stories to the American people, even if those stories contain sensitive national security information. Do you agree with the author's stance? Or is there ever a time when it is better for the American people not to know what the government is doing? Explain your answer thoroughly.

Facts About National Security

Editor's note: These facts can be used in reports or papers to reinforce or add credibility when making important points or claims.

History of National Security in the United States

The modern concept of national security in the United States was introduced after World War II.

President Harry S. Truman signed the National Security Act of 1947 on July 26, 1947. It became the guiding principle of foreign policy in the United States.

James V. Forrestal became the first secretary of defense on September 17, 1947.

The National Security Act and its 1949 amendment established the following departments and agencies:

- The Department of Defense
- Department of the Air Force
- National Security Council
- Central Intelligence Agency

No-Fly Lists

Prior to September 11, 2001, 16 people were deemed by the FBI to be a "suspected threat to aviation" and were not allowed to fly.

The Federal Aviation Administration (FAA) took over responsibility of the list in November 2001. By then, the list had grown to more than 400 names.

By mid-December 2001, the FAA had created two lists: the "No-Fly List," which included 594 people who were denied air transport and the "Selectee" list, which consisted of 365 people who were more carefully searched at airports.

In December 2002 more than 1,000 names were on the No-Fly List.

As of October 2008, the Department of Homeland Security said the No-Fly List contained 2,500 names and the Selectee list contained 16,000 names.

In 2003 President George W. Bush enlisted the FBI and other intelligence agencies to create a "terrorist watch list" of people thought to be terrorists or have terrorist connections. The list is administered by the Terrorist Screening Center and was given to the Transportation Security Administration (TSA) and the commercial airlines. It does not automatically prohibit people from flying but requires they undergo additional scrutiny at airport checkpoints.

As of November 2005, 30,000 people had complained to the TSA that their names were incorrectly included on the terrorist watch list.

A March 2006 copy of the terrorist watch list contained 44,000 names.

As of 2007, the Justice Department said the terrorist watch list contained 700,000 records and was growing by 20,000 records per month.

In 2008 the American Civil Liberties Union (ACLU) estimated the terrorist watch list contained over 1,000,000 names.

In contrast to the ACLU's estimate, the FBI's Terrorist Screening Center said only 400,000 unique names were on the terrorist watch list, explaining that many of the records were duplicates. The FBI also asserted that 95 percent of the people on the list were not U.S. citizens.

National ID Cards and National Security

The REAL ID Act of 2005, a national identification program, was signed into law on May 11, 2005.

All national ID cards in the United States need to contain the following minimum information: the person's full legal name, signature, date of birth, gender, driver's license or identification card number, a photograph, and address.

Many other countries use national ID cards, including Hong Kong, Malaysia, Singapore, Thailand, and most European countries, such as Finland, Belgium, and Germany.

Many states have rejected national ID cards either through law or resolutions. These states include:

- Alaska
- Arkansas
- Colorado
- Georgia

- Hawaii
- Idaho
- Illinois
- Maine
- Missouri
- Montana
- Nebraska
- Nevada
- New Hampshire
- North Dakota
- Oklahoma
- South Carolina
- South Dakota
- Tennessee
- Washington

The Department of Homeland Security has faced so many obstacles with the REAL ID system that the agency extended the implementation deadline to 2017.

Terrorism and Terrorists

In 2005 the FBI did not find a single al Qaeda member in the United States.

According to a 2005 article in the British newspaper the *Independent*, between 100 and 150 suspected terrorists have been arrested and returned to their home country for questioning.

Terrorists typically blend into, and recruit among, co-ethnic immigrant communities. According to the National Intelligence Council, more than 140 million people around the world live outside of their birth countries, and migrants make up more than 15 percent of populations in over fifty countries.

In a 2008 terrorism index survey of more than one hundred foreign policy experts by the Center for American Progress:

- 91 percent of the experts believe the world is becoming more dangerous for Americans and
- 84 percent reported that America is not winning the war on terror.

The National Counterterrorism Center's *2008 Report on Terrorism* revealed the following:

- Of the 11,770 reported attacks, nearly 40 percent occurred in the Near East and 35 percent in South Asia.
- Terrorist kidnappings for ransom increased in 2008. The number of kidnappings rose 45 percent in South Asia, 340 percent in Pakistan, 100 percent in Afghanistan, and 30 percent in India.
- The perpetrators of over 7,000 attacks could not be identified.
- As many as 150 various subnational groups were responsible for the identifiable attacks, including three well-known foreign terrorist organizations.

Nuclear Proliferation

According to the Pentagon, three-quarters of U.S. military assets, from naval bases to nuclear-weapons assembly plants, are found near coastlines. These make ideal targets, not only for enemy rogue nations such as North Korea and Iran, but also for global terrorists.

A report from the bipartisan Commission on the Prevention of Weapons of Mass Destruction (WMD) Proliferation and Terrorism, called *World At Risk*, asserts that "it is more likely than not that a weapon of mass destruction will be used in a terrorist attack somewhere in the world by the end of 2013."

In a 2008 survey of one hundred foreign policy experts:

- 51 percent of respondents thought Pakistan would become the next al Qaeda stronghold;
- 69 percent considered Pakistan to be the most likely country to give nuclear weapons to terrorists in the next three to five years.

The Natural Resources Defense Council estimates there are twenty-two thousand nuclear weapons in the world.

The Nuclear Non-proliferation Treaty

The treaty opened for signature on July 1, 1968.

The treaty was proposed by Ireland.

Finland was the first country to sign.

Currently, 189 countries have signed the treaty. Five of these countries have nuclear weapons—the United States, the United Kingdom, France, Russia, and China.

India, Israel, Pakistan, and North Korea are the only recognized sovereign states to not sign the treaty.

India, Pakistan, and North Korea have declared that they possess nuclear weapons.

North Korea agreed to the treaty, violated it, and then withdrew.

Oil Dependence and National Security
According to the Natural Resources Defense Council, in 2004 America spent more than $200,000 per minute on foreign oil—$13 million per hour. More than $25 billion is spent on oil imports from the Persian Gulf per year.

The United States has less than 5 percent of the world's population but consumes 25 percent of its oil.

Based on projections in 2006, the United States will require almost 30 million barrels of oil per day by the year 2025.

Seventy-six percent of Americans say reducing dependence on foreign oil should be a long-term foreign policy goal.

Climate Change and National Security
Forty percent of Asia's nearly 4 billion people live within forty-five miles of coastlines. This could have a severe effect on national security if sea levels rise as a result of global warming, according to the Center for Naval Analysis.

Fifteen hundred miles of glaciers on the Tibetan Plateau are threatened by climate change, according to GLOBE-EU. These glaciers feed rivers that supply agriculture and drinking water to billions of people in India, Pakistan, and Bangladesh.

According to the Intergovernmental Panel on Climate Change (IPCC), much of the warming in the last century occurred prior to

1940, when human carbon dioxide (CO_2) emissions were relatively small compared with current emissions.

Tree-ring data gathered by scientists studying climate change showed that temperatures in many northern regions from A.D. 950 to 1100 were warmer than temperatures today.

From A.D. 800 to 1300, the Medieval Warm Period, many parts of the world were warmer than they have been in recent decades.

National Security and the Media

A 2007 Pew Research Center study evaluating news leaks about national security found:

- 42 percent of respondents said news leaks are in the best interest of the public because they provide crucial information Americans should know about.
- 44 percent believed news leaks hurt the public interest.
- 26 percent felt that government officials who disclose information to media sources are motivated by personal advancement.
- 12 percent felt that these news leaks were the result of the influence of the press.
- 11 percent felt that officials leaking information to news sources did it for a worthy cause.

Another 2007 Pew Research Center study found that the public is skeptical of the government's complaints about national security press coverage:

- 58 percent felt the government criticizes these stories because it is trying to cover up national security problems.
- 32 percent believe that government is truly concerned that media coverage will harm national security.

National Security and Civil Rights

A 2007 Rasmussen Reports survey found that:

- 34 percent of adults feel that the legal system worries too much about individual rights at the expense of national security.
- 27 percent say there is too much concern for national security.
- 29 percent say the balance is right.

According to the *New York Times*:

- The government's illegal wiretapping program has been used to listen to up to five hundred people at any one time.
- As many as three thousand people may have been spied on between 2002 and 2005.

In 2008 the Supreme Court ruled that wiretapping suspected terrorists without a warrant is legal.

Organizations to Contact

The editors have compiled the following list of organizations concerned with the issues debated in this book. The descriptions are derived from materials provided by the organizations. All have publications or information available for interested readers. The list was compiled on the date of publication of the present volume; the information provided here may change. Be aware that many organizations take several weeks or longer to respond to inquiries, so allow as much time as possible.

American Civil Liberties Union (ACLU)
125 Broad St., 18th Fl.
New York, NY 10004-2400
(212) 549-2500
e-mail: aclu@aclu.org
Web site: www.aclu.org

The ACLU is a national organization that works to defend Americans' civil rights guaranteed by the U.S. Constitution. It argues daily in courts, legislatures, and communities to preserve individual liberties, such as freedom of speech, freedom of the press, and privacy rights. Following the September 2001 terrorist attacks, the ACLU founded its National Security Project, which litigates national security cases involving discrimination, torture, detention, surveillance, and secrecy.

American Enterprise Institute (AEI)
1150 Seventeenth St. NW
Washington, DC 20036
(202) 862-5800
fax: (202) 862-7177
Web site: www.aei.org

The American Enterprise Institute for Public Policy Research is a private, nonpartisan, not-for-profit institution focused on research and education on issues of government, politics, economics, and social welfare. It is dedicated to preserving limited government, private enterprise, and a strong foreign policy and national defense.

The Brookings Institution
1775 Massachusetts Ave. NW
Washington, DC 20036
(202) 797-6000
fax: (202) 797-6004
e-mail: brookinfo@brook.edu
Web site: www.brookings.org

The Brookings Institution is a nonprofit public policy think tank based in Washington, D.C. Comprising over two hundred scholars and experts, the institution conducts independent research in areas of foreign policy, economics, government, and social sciences and provides recommendations that aim to strengthen American democracy, foster economic and social welfare, and create a secure and cooperative international community.

CATO Institute
1000 Massachusetts Ave. NW
Washington, DC 20001-5403
(202) 842-0200
fax: (202) 842-3490
e-mail: cato@cato.org
Web site: www.cato.org

The institute is a nonpartisan public policy research foundation dedicated to limiting the role of government and protecting individual liberties. It publishes the quarterly magazine *Regulation*, the bimonthly *Cato Policy Report*, and numerous policy papers and articles, including many focused on national security.

Center for Defense Information (CDI)
1779 Massachusetts Ave. NW, Ste. 615
Washington, DC 20036
(202) 332-0600
fax: (202) 462-4559
e-mail: info@cdi.org
Web site: www.cdi.org

The CDI is a nonpartisan, nonprofit organization that researches all aspects of global security. It seeks to educate the public and policy makers about issues such as nuclear weapons, security policy, and terrorist threats through its numerous programs, including homeland defense, terrorism, and nuclear proliferation to name a few.

Center for Strategic and International Studies (CSIS)
1800 K St. NW
Washington, DC 20006
(202) 887-0200
fax: (202) 775-3199
e-mail: webmaster@csis.org
Web site: www.csis.org

CSIS is a bipartisan public policy think tank that focuses on America's economic policy, national security, and foreign and domestic policies. The center conducts research and provides strategic insight and policy solutions for government decision makers. It produces ample reports about national security.

Department of Homeland Security (DHS)
U.S. Department of Homeland Security
Washington, DC 20528
(202) 282-8000
Web site: www.dhs.gov

The DHS was created after the September 11, 2001, terrorist attacks. The department seeks to secure the nation while preserving American freedoms and liberties. It is charged with protecting the United States from terrorists, decreasing the country's vulnerability to terrorism, and effectively responding to attacks. The current DHS homeland security strategic plan can be found on its Web site.

Federal Aviation Administration (FAA)
800 Independence Ave. SW
Washington, DC 20591
(866) 835-5322
fax: (202) 267-3484
Web site: www.faa.gov

The FAA is an agency of the U.S. Department of Transportation whose primary responsibility is to maintain civil aviation safety standards. The FAA's major functions include regulating civil aviation to promote safety and fulfill the requirements of national defense.

Institute for Policy Studies (IPS)
1112 Sixteenth St. NW, Ste. 600
Washington, DC 20036
(202) 234-9382
fax: (202) 387-7915
e-mail: info@ips-dc.org
Web site: www.ips-dc.org

The IPS is a nonprofit think tank dedicated to progressive or liberal causes. Founded in 1963, IPS was created to provide independent research and education to address public policy problems in Washington. Its numerous projects are all dedicated to pursuing peace and justice and preserving the environment. Numerous national security reports and papers can be found on its Web site.

Intergovernmental Panel on Climate Change (IPCC)
+41-22-730-8208/84
e-mail: ipcc-sec@wmo.int
Web site: www.ipcc.ch

The IPCC is an international intergovernmental scientific body charged with evaluating the risk of climate change caused by human activity. The panel does not carry out research or monitor climate but rather produces objective reports about climate change based on the latest scientific evidence and literature found in the scientific community. These reports, along with speeches, press releases, and graphic representations, can be found on the IPCC Web site.

National Counterterrorism Center (NCTC)
Web site: www.nctc.gov
The NCTC is charged with analyzing terrorism intelligence, storing terrorism information, and providing lists of terrorists, terrorist groups, and worldwide terrorist incidents to the intelligence community. The NCTC also writes assessments and briefings for policy makers. Its

Web site's Press Room contains press releases, interviews, speeches and testimony, fact sheets, and published reports, as well as the legislation that guides the center's actions.

National Security Agency (NSA)
9800 Savage Rd.
Ft. George Meade, MD 20755
(301) 688-6524
fax: (301) 688-6198
Web site: www.nsa.gov

The NSA is an agency administered by the U.S. Department of Defense. Its main goal is to protect national security systems and to produce foreign intelligence information. The NSA follows U.S. laws to defeat terrorist organizations at home and abroad and ensures the protection of privacy and civil liberties of American citizens. Speeches, congressional testimonies, press releases, and research reports are all available on the NSA Web site.

ProPublica
One Exchange Plaza
55 Broadway, 23rd Fl.
New York, NY 10006
(212) 514-5250
e-mail: info@propublica.org
Web site: www.propublica.org

ProPublica is a nonprofit independent newsroom that produces investigative journalism in the interest of the public. It asserts that investigative journalism is risky but necessary to prevent the exploitation of the weak by the strong and that journalism is a key component of self-government and an important bulwark of American democracy. An entire section of the ProPublica Web site is devoted to national security and contains numerous articles about topics including treatment of terrorist suspects, interrogation techniques, and the NSA's wiretapping program.

Transportation Security Administration (TSA)
601 S. Twelfth St.
Arlington, VA 20598

toll-free: (866) 289-9673
e-mail: tsa-contactcenter@dhs.gov
Web site: www.tsa.gov

The TSA was created in 2001 following the September 11 terrorist attacks and is an agency that serves the U.S. Department of Homeland Security. It is responsible for security in all modes of transportation, including highways, railroads, buses, mass transit systems, ports, and 450 U.S. airports, but particularly aviation security. The TSA has a number of airline security programs, including the Alien Flight Student Program and the Certified Cargo Screening Program, to ensure the safety of the entire airline industry.

Washington Institute for Near East Policy
1828 L St. NW, Ste.1050
Washington, DC 20036
(202) 452-0650
fax: (202) 223-5364
e-mail: info@washingtoninstitute.org
Web site: www.washingtoninstitute.org

The Washington Institute for Near East Policy is an independent think tank that produces research and analysis on U.S.–Middle East policy. It was established to advance a balanced understanding of American interests in the Middle East. It has numerous security programs, including the Stein Program on Counterterrorism and Intelligence and the Military and Security Studies Program.

For Further Reading

Books

Bush, George W. *National Strategy for Combating Terrorism*. Garden City, NY: Morgan James, 2009.

Campbell, Kurt M. *Climatic Cataclysm: The Foreign Policy and National Security Implications of Climate Change*. Washington, DC: Brookings Institution, 2008.

Clarke, Richard A. *Your Government Failed You: Breaking the Cycle of National Security Disasters*. New York: Ecco, 2008.

Gray, Colin S. *National Security Dilemmas: Challenges and Opportunities*. Dulles, VA: Potomac, 2009.

Harrison, John. *International Aviation and Terrorism: Evolving Threats, Evolving Security*. New York: Routledge, 2009.

Myers, Richard B. *Eyes on the Horizon: Serving on the Front Lines of National Security*. New York: Threshold, 2009.

Preble, Christopher A. *The Power Problem: How American Military Dominance Makes Us Less Safe, Less Prosperous, and Less Free*. Ithaca, NY: Cornell University Press, 2009.

Sarkesian, Sam C., John Allen Williams, and Stephen J. Cimbala. *US National Security: Policymakers, Processes and Politics*. Boulder, CO: Lynne Rienner, 2007.

Schreier, Fred. *WMD Proliferation: Reforming the Security Sector to Meet the Threat*. Dulles, VA: Potomac, 2009.

Stuart, Douglas T. *Creating the National Security State: A History of the Law That Transformed America*. Princeton, NJ: Princeton University Press, 2008.

Walker, William O., III. *National Security and Core Values in American History*. West Nyack, NY: Cambridge University Press, 2009.

Periodicals and Internet Sources

Ashton, John. "World's Most Wanted: Climate Change," BBC,

September 8, 2006. http://news.bbc.co.uk/2/hi/science/nature/5323 512.stm.

Black, Nicole. "Commentary: Does Security Require the Loss of Liberty?" *Rochester (NY) Daily Record*, August 18, 2008.

Bovard, James. "Our Dangerous Times," *American Conservative*, July 31, 2006. www.amconmag.com/article/2006/jul/31/00020/.

Campbell, Kurt M. et al. "The Age of Consequences: The Foreign Policy and National Security Implications of Global Climate Change," Center for New American Security, November 2007. www.csis.org/media/csis/pubs/071105 _ageofconsequences.pdf.

Dalmia, Shikha. "Defend America, Buy More Iranian Oil," Reason Foundation, May 5, 2006. www.reason.org/commentaries/dalmia_ 20060505.shtml.

Dreyfuss, Robert. "The Phony War," *Rolling Stone*, September 11, 2006. www.rollingstone.com/politics/story/11598509/national_ affairs_president_bushs_phony_war_on_terror/print.

———— . "There Is No War on Terror," TomPaine.com, September 11, 2006. www.tompaine.com/articles/2006/09/13/there_is_no_ war_on_terror.php.

Franklin, Sharon Bradford, and Sarah Holcomb. "Watching the Watch Lists: Maintaining Security and Liberty in America," *Human Rights*, Summer 2007.

Kaplan, Eben. "American Muslims and the Threat of Homegrown Terrorism," Council on Foreign Relations, May 8, 2007. www.cfr .org/publication/11509/.

Kingsbury, Alex. "How the Al Qaeda Terrorism Threat Is Mutating," *U.S. News & World Report*, November 14, 2008. www.usnews .com/articles/news/iraq/2008/11/14/how-the-al-qaeda-terrorism-threat-is-mutating.html.

Larkin, Erik. "Coming Soon: National ID Cards? Recently Passed Real ID Act Undermines Civil Rights, Critics Charge," *PC World*, May 31, 2005. www.pcworld.com/article/121077/coming_soon_ national_id_cards.html.

Little, Amanda Griscom. "Will Global Warming Threaten National Security?" Salon.com, April 9, 2007. www.salon.com/news/feature/ 2007/04/09/muckraker/.Heather.

Martin, Liam. "On the Government's Power in Matters of National Security," *American Chronicle*, June 28, 2007. www.americanchronicle .com/articles/view/30921.

Mueller, John. "Is There Still a Terrorist Threat? The Myth of the Omnipresent Enemy," *Foreign Affairs*, September/October 2006.

Potter, Andrew. "If Security Fails, There Is Always a Scapegoat: Freedom—Why the Relationship Between Freedom and Security Doesn't Have to Be See-Saw," *Maclean's*, September 12, 2006. www .macleans.ca/columnists/article.jsp?content=20060911_132943_12943.

Ritter, Scott. "The Big Lie: 'Iran Is a Threat,'" Common Dreams.org, October 8, 2007. www.commondreams.org/archive/2007/10/08/ 4404.

Roper, Mary Catherine. "Liberty for Security: How Is That Trade Working for You?" *Legal Intelligencer*, January 22, 2007.

Rotenberg, Marc. "Privacy vs. Security? Privacy," *HuffingtonPost*, November 9, 2007. www.huffingtonpost.com/marc-rotenberg/privacy -vs-security-pr_b_71806.html.

Schneier, Bruce. "The Eternal Value of Privacy," *Wired*, May 18, 2006. www.wired.com/politics/security/commentary/securitymatters/20 06/05/70886.

———. "What Our Top Spy Doesn't Get: Security and Privacy Aren't Opposites," *Wired*, January 24, 2008. www.wired.com/politics/security/ commentary/securitymatters/2008/01/securitymatters_0124?current Page=all&.

Scire, John. "Oil Dependency, National Security," *Nevada Appeal*, February 10, 2008. www.nevadaappeal.com/article/20080210/ OPINION/227691244.

Tallen, Bill. "Paramilitary Terrorism: A Neglected Threat," *Homeland Security Affairs*, vol. 4, no.2, June 2008. www.hsai.org/?fullarticle =4.2.6.

Trent, Brian. "National ID Card Threatens Security," Populist America.com, April 15, 2007. www.populistamerica.com/national_ id_card_threatens_security.

Walsh, Bryan. "Does Global Warming Compromise National Security?" *Time*, April 16, 2008. www.time.com/time/specials/2007/ article/0,28804,1730759_1731383_1731632,00.html.

Zuckerman, Mortimer B. "Putting Safety First," *U.S. News & World Report*, July 16, 2007.

Web Sites

The American Civil Defense Association (TACDA) (www.tacda.org). The American Civil Defense Association was formed in the 1960s in response to America's increasing reliance on atomic weapons in foreign policy. The TACDA strives to inform both the military and the private sector about civil defense awareness and disaster preparedness for all types of disasters, including nuclear, biological, chemical, and natural disasters.

Center for a New American Security (CNAS) (www.cnas.org). Founded in 2007, this independent nonpartisan research institution develops national security and defense policies that promote and protect American values and interests. CNAS provides policy makers, experts, and the public with fact-based research and analysis to guide the national security debate.

Memorial Institute for the Prevention of Terrorism (MIPT) (www.mipt.org). This nonprofit counterterrorism center uses analysis, training, and information sharing to prevent terrorist attacks. Formed in response to the 1995 Oklahoma City bombing, MIPT is supported by the Department of Homeland Security. MIPT maintains the MIPT Terrorist Knowledge Base, which is an online database of terrorist groups, leaders, incidents, related court cases, and other information.

UnRealID.com (www.unrealid.com). This site is devoted to opposing the REAL ID Act, which was passed by Congress in 2005. The REAL ID Act turns driver's licenses into national ID cards and requires citizens to compile all their personal data in one place. The site urges citizens to contact their senators and tell them to oppose the REAL ID Act.

Index

information technology and, 101
numbers of, 15
poses serious threat to national
  security, 12–17
Saudi Arabia and, 27–28, 34
survey of foreign policy experts
  on likelihood of, *16*
See also War on terror
Terrorist Screening Database
  (TSDB), 84, 85
Time (magazine), 136
Transportation Security
  Administration, U.S. (TSA),
  84–88

U
United States
  changes in coast line, *43*
  climate change and, 42–43
  oil imports by, *28*
  oil-producing countries and, *34*
  role in Persian Gulf, 26
  sources of oil imports, 33, *35*
  See also Military, U.S.; National
    security
U.S. Constitution, 106–107

V
Van Doren, Peter, 31

W
Wall Street Journal (newspaper),
  130, 131
War on terror
  false alarms in, *21*
  requires surveillance, 100–101
Washington Post (newspaper),
  125
Water resources, 41–42
  climate change as threat to,
    42–43
  migration from Mexico and, 44
Watkins, Sharon, 136
Wiretapping
  of Americans illegally, 75–82
  keeps U.S. safe, 69–74
  National Security Agency's
    program for, 133–134
Wirth, Timothy, 48–49
Wright, Lawrence, 62

Z
al-Zawahiri, Ayman, 63
Zilmer, Richard, 29

Picture Credits

Maury Aaseng, 16, 21, 28, 35, 39, 53, 65, 87, 93, 102, 121, 126, 139
AP Images, 14, 27, 34, 43, 55, 62, 67, 73, 81, 85, 91, 96, 99, 119
© Caro/Alamy, 115
Kevin Dietsch/UPI/Landov, 125
Yuri Gripas/Reuters/Landov, 137
Sheng Li/Reuters/Landov, 47
© MasPix/Alamy, 11
National Gallery of Art/Time & Life Pictures/Getty Images, 109
PA Photos/Landov, 20
© Martin Shields/Alamy, 131